Sefer Yetzirah

Ultimate Guide to Understanding the Earliest Extant Work on Jewish Mysticism that Was Mentioned in the Talmud

Your Free Gift (only available for a limited time)

Thanks for getting this book! If you want to learn more about various spirituality topics, then join Mari Silva's community and get a free guided meditation MP3 for awakening your third eye. This guided meditation mp3 is designed to open and strengthen ones third eye so you can experience a higher state of consciousness. Simply visit the link below the image to get started.

https://spiritualityspot.com/meditation

Contents

Introduction

The Sefer Yetzirah (Book of Formation) has attracted intense study and debate for centuries. Without a doubt, it is one of the most formative texts in the canon of Jewish religious literature.

The earliest existing book of the Kabbalah authorship is debated to this day. Many date Sefer Yetzirah to the Middle Ages, but others insist it was produced in its earliest form in the 2nd Century CE. The form of Hebrew in the earliest iteration of the text seems to point to the latter.

But tradition, of course, ascribes authorship to a chain of oral transmission beginning with Adam, Primordial Man. From Adam, Sefer Yetzirah was passed to Noah and then to Abraham. The intimation is that the book was given to humanity in the Garden of Eden and is of Divine authorship.

This is in keeping with the esoteric content of Sefer Yetzirah, which we'll explore in this book. We'll meet the probable author of this detailed description of how the world around us came to be and explore the book's complex prescriptions and narratives toward a better understanding.

Join me now, as we enter the world of Kabbalah's foundational expression – the mystical Sefer Yetzirah.

Chapter One: A Mystic's Guide to Creation

Referred to in Talmudic sources as "Otiyyot de-Avraham Avinu" (Letters of Abraham, our Father), the Sefer Yetzirah is traditionally considered as part of the Oral Torah delivered to Moses at Sinai.

The idea of Oral Tradition in Judaism is key here. While "authorship" is ascribed to the Patriarch, Abraham, the concept casts God as depositing certain key knowledge with key figures in the Bible to be written down later. In this tradition, the knowledge of the Divine is passed through notable emissaries through the ages, mouth to ear.

Anyone who's ever played the game of "telephone" understands that the way of Oral History is fraught with peril. What is transmitted to the original ear may take on rather a lot of baggage once it's been transmitted by thousands of mouths to thousands of ears. Distortions, amendments, omissions, and errors may occur. But the place of Oral Tradition is Judaism comes with an enduring commitment to codification, study, and interpretation, and so "telephone" meets its match.

Direct Revelation of God – The Oral Torah

The Oral Tradition's significance and power in the Jewish Faith is perhaps even greater than that of the written tradition. It stands apart from the revered corpus of Jewish literature as its Divine origin – the direct revelation of God to Israel's people.

From the Oral Tradition comes the tradition of the Sabbath – which, while mentioned in the Torah, comes with few traditions prescribing its celebration there. Similarly, items of religious apparel institutionalized in the practice of Judaism, like the tefillin (phylacteries) and tzitzit (fringed prayer shawl), are mentioned in Torah, with the specifics about their form and use extrapolated from Oral Tradition.

Because of these "gaps" in Tanakh (the written tradition), the Oral Tradition is what drives interpretation and practice. So, it functions as a guide to the student, through the support of the teacher, who has received the Oral Tradition. Questions about interpretation are funneled through this control mechanism to ensure accurate interpretation of the written record.

This tradition functions to ensure that the Torah's Divine origin, as delivered in its primordial form, is never misinterpreted and thus, does not deviate from the Divine Will, transmitted to Moses.

The written Torah, subject to the glosses, redactions, and the varying interpretations of millions, has in the Oral Torah, a litmus test, based on the purest form of the game of telephone – God's revelation to Moses, from the Divine mouth to the Prophet's ear.

This factor is crucial to understanding why the Sefer Yetzirah's authorship continues to be a point of vigorous contention for scholars. There's no "byline" that accompanies Divine revelation. But from the moment we're able to pinpoint a written location, we're able to start putting the pieces of the written record together.

Origins of the Written Text

While scholars continue to disagree on authorship, a consensus agrees that the original, written content can be traced to the work of Rabbi Akiva ben Yosef (50 CE - 135 CE.) He was a robust contributor to the texts of Mishnah (meaning "rote learning" from the study), that is the later codification of the cumulative Oral Tradition. But even in this version, the text is attributed to Abraham via the folkloric interpretation of transmission.

This dating was arrived at by examining the use of language in the text against the form of Hebrew native to the 2nd Century CE and tracing Rabbi Akiva's work through the Mishnah. While this attribution is not globally accepted in the academic world, it is the most common, and so we will accept it for our journey into Sefer Yetzirah's mysteries.

There are multiple versions of the text, produced over time, of which the four most referenced are:

- A brief version
- A long-form version
- The Saadia version
- The Gra version

While containing minor deviations, all versions are materially the same. The brief version is 1,300 words long, while the long form is just under 3,000 words.

The Saadia version, named for a commentary on the Sefer Yetzirah from the 10th Century by the Saadia Gaon (circa 892 - 942 CE), is a differently organized version of the long-form. Finally, the Gra version is derived from the work of Isaac Luria (1534 - 1572 CE) on the short version to align it with the Zohar. This version was then redacted by the Vilna Gaon (1720 - 1797 CE, who was called the "Gra"), becoming the Gra version.

But Sefer Yetzirah's appearance in the Talmud is the true backbone of dating the text to the Second Century. So, our next commission in the apprehension of understanding Sefer Yetzirah is to understand the Talmud's meaning and historical setting.

Talmud (Mishnah and Gemara)

The backbone of Rabbinical Judaism is from the Talmud; from which the halakha (Jewish Law) is derived. The Talmud is also the primary source for Jewish theology. In essence, it is also the Talmud, which serves as the backbone for daily Jewish life.

This body of Jewish religious literature is huge, comprising the Babylonian Talmud (Talmud Bavli). This collection is divided between the Mishnah (c. 200 CE), that is the Oral Torah, the Gemara (c. 500), which elaborates further on Mishnah, and writings from the Tannaitic period (c. 10 – 200 CE – also called the Mishnaic period).

Written in the Hebrew of the Tannaitic/Mishnaic period and Aramaic of Babylonian times, the Talmud compiles the teachings and interpretations of many thousands of sages, starting from Oral Tradition, which dates to before the Common Era. These teachings include everything from halakha to ethics to philosophy, folklore, and customs, among myriad topics of discussion and debate by the learned of the Jewish community.

Jerusalem Talmud (Talmud Yerushalmi)

Also known as the Palestinian or Talmuda de-Eretz Yisrael (Talmud of the Land of Israel), the Jerusalem Talmud offers commentaries on the Mishnah. The bulk of this text was written in Galilee, in both Hebrew and Palestinian Aramaic.

Like its later Babylonian counterpart, the Jerusalem Talmud contains Mishnah and Gemara, but the Gemara is how it differs most from that later version, as it includes the teachings of the sages of the

Holy Land (mostly in Tiberias and Caesarea), finally compiled between 350 and 400 BC.

The Babylonian Talmud is considered the more authoritative of the two, being distributed widely during the Middle Ages. When there is divergence about halakha between the two, the Babylonian Talmud is followed. Large portions of the Jerusalem Talmud were lost.

In the middle of the 4th Century CE, the Romans forcibly suppressed scholarship among Israeli Jews, and so they escaped to Babylon. Without colonialist interference, the Babylon Talmud became the more authoritative text.

Mentioned multiple times in the Babylonian Talmud, the earliest reference to Sefer Yetzirah occurs in Haggah 12a, dated to the year 70 CE.

Philosophy or Mysticism?

Considered the earliest example of Kabbalistic literature, the interpretation of Sefer Yetzirah is divided into two streams. The first is philosophical, rooted in mathematics and language. The second is mystical, rooted in the same features of the text.

Since the Middle Ages, scholars have examined and studied Sefer Yetzirah. The general rule of the commentaries - produced from these explorations - is that the scholars of the Middle Ages arrived at *philosophical* conclusions, while later scholars arrived at *mystical* ones.

Saadia Gaon (882 - 942 CE) takes the philosophical approach, comparing elements of Greek philosophy with Hebrew thought encountered in Sefer Yetzirah. Judah Halevi (1080 - 1142 CE), while acknowledging the philosophical component, reaches toward the mystical to demonstrating the primacy of Hebrew spirituality in the text.

But a key to understanding Sefer Yetzirah is the power of the spoken Word of God, as contained in the Creation narrative of Genesis. For example, in Genesis 1:3, "And God said, 'let there be light,' and there was light." At the beginning of Sefer Yetzirah is the statement that God had "engraved with thirty-two paths of wisdom and created his world". That engraving was of the living Word, carried on the breath of God as the creative force.

The name of the book itself is a strong clue as to its intentions, regarding how Creation is wrought. The Hebrew word "yetzirah" is commonly translated as "creation." But more properly translated, it is "formation." In the story of Creation, matter is formed at the Creator's will and becomes what it was created to do. This speaks to the idea of "ayin" (nothingness, which *is something*) in regard to the constructs in play, namely, the sefirot (which we'll discuss at length a little later.) Ayin is the state of Creation before the Word of God was spoken to "form" it, as described in Genesis 1:2, "the earth was a formless void, and darkness covered the face of the deep." (NB: Oxford NRSV Bible quoted throughout).

The formless raw material is there, asleep to its purpose in ayin, where nothingness awaiting its birth into "somethingness." As the final wording of Genesis 1:2 says, "While a wind from God swept over the face of the waters." As the creative force in play, God takes the raw material, creating from it the final form it was intended to take.

In this respect, Creation, as explicated by Sefer Yetzirah, is philosophically advanced. The idea of a Creation made from existing materials aligns with the thinking of Parmenides, founder of metaphysics in Greek philosophy, who wrote, "ex nihilo nihil fit" (from nothing comes nothing). This idea permeated Greek cosmology and was first quoted in Aristotle's Physics.

And it's the formation of matter with which Sefer Yetzirah is chiefly concerned. In its model, creation is a building project using "formless" raw material held in the void of ayin. The influence of Greek philosophy on the text is clear and to be expected in the cauldron of thought; it was created in the Ancient Near East. Especially when we consider the original document's presumed authorship, usually attributed to the Safed sage, Rabbi Akiva; his location in the Middle East would have exposed him to that cauldron and its bubbling mix of regional thought.

So, while the influence of Greek philosophy is clear, so is the book's mystical intention. There is no rule stating that philosophy and mysticism can't coexist. In fact, philosophy and mysticism complement one another rather abundantly.

In a confrontation of philosophy's rationalism, mysticism does not provide access to another level of apprehending reality, which is spiritual but not at all devoid of intellect. Rather, mysticism points to direct access to and experience of the Divine's presence in reality as an intellectual superpower, an intellect infused with the Spirit of the Creator, reaching through our pallid apprehension of reality to what is not rationally explained but which must be known for the intellect to be whole and balanced.

Disagreement and Controversy - Dating and Authorship

Accompanying the intense study of Sefer Yetzirah is the debate surrounding authorship and the dating of the book. While the traditional origin is in the Oral Tradition, traced back to the deposit of God's Word in Primordial Man (Adam) and then, through the Prophets and Patriarchs, a human hand transcribed what had been orally transmitted.

And to this date, the debate rages on. There is even a school of thought which dates Sefer Yetzirah to the Middle Ages. But others say, because of the influence of Jewish agnosticism, the book was originally written in the 3rd or 4th Century. Certainly, this branch of Judaism had all but disappeared by the end of the 4th Century, CE.

There is one school of thought which places Sefer Yetzirah's written origin in the 2nd Century BCE.

But most scholars today agree that the written text can be dated to the 2nd Century, during the Mishnaic/Tannaitic period (10 – 220 CE). The use of the Hebrew language in the text most closely resembles the written form of the language in use at the time.

Many manuscripts of the Sefer Yetzirah are inscribed with the words, "The Letter of Abraham, our Father, which is called Sefer Yetzirah." But his authorship has been disputed for centuries, notably by Moses Cordovero (1522 – 1570). Cordovero, a student of Isaac Luria and later, a renowned Miggdal (Kabbalah Master), wrote in Pardes Rimmon, "There are those who attribute (Sefer Yetzirah) to Rabbi Akiva, but the latter is not the accepted opinion." Cordovero supports this assertion by saying that Abraham had written the book and that Akiva had only redacted it. And it's certainly the case that text has been added, subtracted, and tinkered with over many centuries. This practice continues today.

The fact that the Sefer Yetzirah is mentioned either directly or indirectly in the Babylon Talmud as early as 70 BC supports an earlier appearance of a written document. The Talmudic references are specifically to the use of the book to create life, as it was used to create the various *golemim* (a humanoid creature made from clay, animated by magic) of the Hassidim later on.

While the debate continues, the overall opinion of those who've studied the book is that it dates to the 2nd Century CE. Further, Moses Cordovero, notwithstanding, Akiva is the most likely author, even if his efforts were limited to an existing text's redaction. For the time being, that's the closest Jewish academia has gotten to the whole truth.

Structure and Themes

The Sefer Yetzirah is primarily concerned with the mechanics of Creation, presenting its major themes:

- 32 paths of wisdom are delineated
- Creation is presented as a manifestation of God's name
- Creation's nature is three-fold
- The aleph bet (Hebrew alphabet) is God in Creation
- The Tree of Life
- Yesh m'yesh (that something comes from something, as opposed to "from nothing" or ex nihilo nihil fit – from nothing comes nothing)
- Creation via transformation and permutation of existing matter
- Techniques for meditation

The unique features of Sefer Yetzirah present a different layer of interpretation and study. One of the most striking is the employment of mathematics and language as divine agents in the creative process, representing a unique cosmological viewpoint.

So, our next chapter will approach these themes, as well as discussing the book's structure and chapter breakdown. We'll also find out how Sefer Yetzirah connects with the Book of Ecclesiastes in the Hebrew Scriptures.

Chapter Two: Into the Mysteries

As we've discussed in the earlier chapter, the four principal versions of the Sefer Yetzirah are substantially the same, except for the long-form version, that contains commentary, accounting for its length next to the brief version.

Chapters

The book is organized into six chapters, with supplements to chapters 4 and 5, and begins with an exploration of the ten cardinal numbers and 22 letters, describing their roles in the creative process. Chapter 2 goes into more detail, with the earthly elements and the "mother letters," aleph, mem, and shin mentioned, and the letters of the aleph-bet, as constituting the One God.

Chapter 3 describes the role of the mother letters in concert with the earthly elements in the creative process. Chapter 4 is an elaboration on the seven doubles (see below) and their interaction with the opposing forces extant in Creation, and an exposition of the significance of the number 7, with the supplement (commentary) elaborating further and ascribing qualities like beauty, peace, wisdom, and health to each.

Chapter 5 describes the work of the elemental or simple letters (see below) as forming the Constellations of the Zodiac and corresponding to the properties of the number 7 as it occurs in sources from Hebrew Scriptures and to the days of the week. The accompanying commentary ascribes bodily functions and human emotions to each of the elemental/simple letters. (NB: these are assigned differently in later commentaries). Chapter 6 again describes the word of the elements in concert with the mother letters, introducing the "celestial dragon" and three-pronged nature of Creation. Finally, the Word is relayed to Abraham, who promptly transcribes and makes the Covenants of the hands and feet with God.

A Technical and Mystical Description of Creation

Sefer Yetzirah's purpose is to provide a technical and mystical description of God's creative process, resulting in all we know and all we are. In the first sentence, we listed all of God's names, which stand in the book as the "32 wondrous ways of wisdom." These have been "engraved" on the Created Order. This implies that all that the Divine has created is the manifestation of those names. This is not so much "Divine graffiti" as an exposition of God's immanence in what's been created. This reference is parallel to Proverbs 3:19, which states, "The LORD by wisdom founded the earth."

The values of the 32 ways of wisdom are divided into several categories:

- The sefirot (which we'll be discussing in detail shortly) are described in this text as 10 numbers.
- The Hebrew aleph-bet is described as twenty-two letters.
- Aleph, Mem and Shin, are described as the three mother letters of the aleph-bet.

• Bet, Gimel, Dalet, Kaph, Pe, Resh and Tau are described as the seven doubles.

• He, Vav, Zayin, Het, Tet, Yud, Lamed, Nun, Samekh, Ayin, Tzady, and Kuf, are described as the 12 elementals or simples.

These designations align with concepts in Jewish theology like the composition of the Tetragrammaton (YHVH) from three letters – yud, hey, and vav. The number 7 describes the sabbatical structure of Jewish time in the religious and ethical practice of Judaism. It refers to the Sabbatical structure of the week and the cycle of agriculture, in which the land rests in the seventh year. The 12 Tribes of Israel, the 12 gates granting access to the Temple in Jerusalem, and the sons of Jacob, are all examples of the prominence of the number 12 in the Hebrew Scriptures. As readers will be aware, this was carried forward into Christianity in the 12 Apostles of Jesus (deliberately selected in that number to represent the 12 Tribes).

But again, we seek the influence of early science in the numbers in play. For example, the four elements of Creation (earth, fire, air, and water), the seven planets, and the 12 constellations of the zodiac. Also, in play is how the number 10 (the sefirot) relates to the human body, for example:

• The number 10 is expressed on the human body in the 10 toes of the feet, which relates to ceremonial circumcision. In Hebrew, this is called "mila," which may also be translated as "word." Specifically, the reference in Sefer Yetzirah refers to the spaces between the toes.

• This number is also expressed in the 10 fingers on the hands, corresponding to language's covenant. The Hebrew word is "lashon," which means both "language" and "tongue." Again, the reference is to the space between the digits of the hand, as with the feet and mila.

Sefer Yetzirah ends with God connecting the 22 letters of Hebrew (essentially described as the Torah, itself, in the book) to Abraham's own tongue, referring directly to the transmission of esoteric knowledge to the Patriarch.

The 10 Sefirot

In Sefer Yetzirah, we find one of Kabbalistic literature's first references to the sefirot, described as "ten numbers." Interpreting the word is multifarious due to the root letters of the words "sefirah" (singular) and "sefirot" (plural). Described in the text as "nothingness" or "ineffable," the word also appears in the Babylonian Talmud (B. Menachot 65b) but describes the counting of the "omer" (a unit of measurement, applied to the counting of raw stalks of wheat). The usage suggests that the word, in this instance, is "sefar," which means "number."

Due to the absence of vowels in the Hebrew language (later indicated by "pointings" or symbols denoting vowels), the meaning of words is largely determined by context and a thorough understanding of the use of root consonants. Here, the root is samekh, pey, resh, indicating several possibilities:

- Sefar – number
- Sefer – written record; book
- Sifur – telling or communication

At the end of the first verse of Sefer Yetzirah, we encounter all three words – sefar, sefer, and sifur, stating that the world was created with text, numbers, and communication.

The "10 sefirot of nothingness," also translates as the "10 ineffable sefirot" suggesting their nature as beyond the human understanding and thus, the likeness of God, creating from the void. This suggests the formlessness of a world not yet ordered by the Divine word, as read in Genesis 1:3 "the earth was a formless void." Another Biblical reference of interest in this question is found in Ecclesiastes 1:2, which reads, "Vanity of vanities, says the Teacher, vanity of vanities! All is vanity."

The word "vanity" here is "*hevel*" or "*havel*" in Hebrew. This is sometimes translated as "futility." More common, though, is the translation "vanity" (which also means vapor or steam – dehiscence, the process of becoming immaterial through evaporation).

When we encounter the word in the Sefer Yetzirah, it implies that the matter from which God creates is "*hevel*" or "vapor/dehiscence" and, thus, a grand illusion.

Why 32?

Some scholars attribute the number 32 to an effort on the part of the author of Sefer Yetzirah to harmonize two specific instances in Talmud. Namely, that found in B. Berachot 55a, "Bezalel (credited with building the Temple in Exodus 31: 1 – 6 and Exodus 36 – 39) knew how to combine the letters by which the heavens and earth were created" and in Pirkei Avot 5:1, "With 10 utterances was the world created".

These nine explicit examples are found in the Creation narrative of Genesis, where the words "and God said," occur in the text 10 times, with one implicit instance.

This is based on an exegetical source found in Psalm 33:6 and interpreted in the Talmud, in B. Megilah 21b. "The words 'in the beginning' are also an utterance, since it is written, "By the word of the LORD, the heavens were made, and all their host by the breath of his mouth" (Psalm 33:6).

As we've read earlier, the covenants of circumcision and of the word are related to the spaces between the toes and fingers, respectively. In like manner, the number 32 has a physical application. The number of vertebrae in the spine is 32, as is the number of permanent teeth.

And in the Creation narrative, the name of God, "Elohim," is mentioned 32 times. What the number, as a composite of the letters of the Hebrew aleph-bet and the 10 numbers (sefirot) reveals is that the "32 ways of wisdom" engraved on Creation are a rendering of the Holy Name of God into 32 constituent pieces, which are, in truth, but One. But because "God is One" (from the Shemah, the Jewish daily prayer, "Shemah, Israel! Adonai eloheynu, Adonai Echad" (Hear, O Israel! The Lord our God, the LORD is One!), the "nothingness" of the 10 sefirot refers directly to the illusory nature of the Created Order.

Creation as the Name of God

In our exploration of Creation as the name of God, we'll turn to the later Kabbalistic document, the Zohar.

Comparing the Sefer Yetzirah and how it correlates to Zohar demonstrates the growth of Jewish thought through time. But we also know that later manuscripts of the Sefer Yetzirah were to harmonize its content with that of Zohar.

Identified as the home of the name of God, "Elohim," the sefirah Binah (understanding) shares the honor with sefirah Malkhut (sovereignty). This last sefirah is also known as Shekhinah (Divine Presence).

Internationally recognized Kabbalah scholar, Gershom Scholem, posited there is no difference in the Talmud, between Shekhinah and YHVH. But in Sefer ha Bahir, the notion of Shekhinah being somehow separated from the Divine, gave rise to the King's Divine model (Elohim) and his Daughter (Shekhinah).

In the revelation of Divine Presence, embodied in Shekhinah, we encounter the Divine as a revelation of YHVH, a Divine name. Indwelling the Created Order, the Divine Presence reveals the Divine's true nature, immanent in Creation.

This Divine Presence making the nature of God known in Creation is temporary. While God is One, Divine unity is sacrificed to show forth God's glory. But when the Created Order is cleansed of all evil and the Moshiach (Messiah) returns, Shekhinah will again be one with the Divine source from which it emanates as a sefirah. This relates to tzimtzum – the breaking of the vessels and the contraction of the Divine to make room for Creation (see Chapter Four).

God's names permeate and transform the raw material from which God spoke into being the Created Order. But at the root of this power is language. As we've seen in the Creation narrative, God's breath, bearing the creative invocations, utilizes the Hebrew language to bring forth the whole of Creation, both infusing it and engraving it, even "stamping" it (via the sefirot) with the Divine Presence of the Daughter, Shekhinah.

While our discussion of the sefirot a little later in this book will go into detail, for our purposes here, each of the 10 sefirot on the Tree of Life (Etz Chaim) correspond to a name of God. In their emanation from the godhead, they transport the Holy Name through this creative agency, in all its forms.

Three-Fold Creation and the Name

Aleph, mem, and shin are the three mother letters of Creation. Each letter corresponds to a physical element. Mem corresponds to water, shin, fire, and aleph to air. Take a moment to consider the phonetic property of the letters. Mem is "m" – a hum, like the sound of a river. Shin is "sh," like the sound of a fire crackling, and aleph is an avocal (silent) letter. While having tremendous weight in the aleph-bet, it also makes no sound – like air.

In the human body, the head is the fire of shin, the belly is the water of mem, and the chest is the air of aleph.

These three mother letters serve to define the work of the aleph-bet, mediating between the Created elements, God, and humanity. But it's the letter shin that is most evocative of the idea of a three-fold Creation, in its graphic form.

The three prongs of the letter, which rise from the cup formed by the letter's base, stand as an icon of the pattern of the number 3 in Sefer Yetzirah. It stands as a glyph representing knowledge as three-fold, embodied in the one who knows what is known, and the actual work of knowing.

But like the Created Order in the model of Sefer Yetzirah, shin also represents an illusion. Like a coal-burning, the fire produced from the raw material is not separate from its combustible source. Like the diversity of Creation, encompassed by one sole manifestation of the Divine, the burning coal expresses division into three while existing in complete unity.

"The LORD is one," affirmed in the Shema and repeatedly propounded throughout Jewish literature. The number 3 in the Created Order represents Creation's expression as a manifestation of the Divine, just as the letter shin is but one letter and not three.

And we can dive *even deeper* into the esoteric meaning of the three mother letters and their communal representation of the name of God. Consider, for a moment, the phonetic properties of the three – mmm, shhhh, and silence. Shin and mem, when spoken, result in the world "shem" – name (meaning specifically, the name of God when spoken as "ha Shem" – the name).

As for the silent partner in this cosmic conspiracy of 3, aleph, due to its graphic form, may be "taken apart," resulting in two yuds and a vav (h, h, u). When this is done, the numeric value comes into play, and the resulting value - when the three letters are added - is 26; that is the number value of the Tetragrammaton. In Zohar 1: 16a, YHVH is described as "sheer silence."

For a moment, let's return to the first verse of Sefer Yetzirah and sefar (number), sefer (book), sifur (communication). With these three "books," the Created Order came into being, highlighting the tension between opposites in the Universe as the source of balance or homeostasis (the state of balance and optimal functioning in all life). In the model presented in Sefer Yetzirah, that balance is inherent to the creative agency of the 22 letters and 1o numbers, facilitated by the dialogue between them.

Ecclesiastes 7:14 offers a locus classicus for this balance/tension between opposites, which is passionately apprehended in Sefer Yetzirah, saying, "Also God made one opposite the other." This indicates a strong tendency to equate the energy between opposites with homeostatic balance. In other words - a healthy, well-adjusted Creation.

What's remarkable is that the concept of balance and tension is richly realized in Sefer Yetzirah, but also throughout the canon of Jewish religious literature. In the realm of Physics, as in that of Jewish philosophy/exegetical discipline, tension is the state of strain that occurs when opposing forces pull against each other, as in a tug-o-war. But that tug-o-war, in the context of Jewish religious traditions, indicates a "holding together" more than a pulling apart.

And a big part of that balancing act is the Etz Chaim, the Tree of Life that is the icon of the combined sefirot.

Chapter Three: The Sefirot

The Tree of Life is Etz Chaim, with many incarnations in both the Hebrew and Christian Scriptures. It's described in the Book of Genesis as "in the midst of the Garden of Eden" (Genesis 2: 9). But in the Sefer Yetzirah, Etz Chaim stands as the primordial organization of God's sefirot (emanations; attributes).

This subject is deep and broad, so I'll present a picture as full as I can, exploring the philosophically and spiritually dense body of thought arising from the sefirot in Sefer Yetzirah and their specific role in the model of Creation the book expounds.

The complexity of Kabbalistic thinking, writing, and inquiry around the sefirot is daunting, but knowing a little more about where the sefirot came from, both spiritually and historically, and what their story is in the literature will bring us a little further along in the journey.

The Inner Soul of Torah

Isaac Luria once described Kabbalah as the "inner soul" of the Torah. By honoring the white space around the letters and the letters themselves, Kabbalah reads not just between the lines of Torah but beneath them, layer by careful layer. And what results is a mystical vision that unites philosophical rigor to spiritual experience. While we'll be sticking to discussing the sefirot in this chapter, we'll be touching on the features of linguistic mysticism and gematria and their importance in Sefer Yetzirah here. A more thorough treatment of these will take place in Chapter Seven. But this book is so infused with these two elements that they will pop up here and there before we've had an opportunity to examine them. I hope the sefirot will whet your appetite!

As Torah's inner soul, Kabbalah tells a tale of yearning for Creation. Neither here nor there, something or nothing, good or evil, the good intentions of God did not meet their intended end.

That is not to say that Creation is not "very good," as declared by God in Genesis 1:31. It is carefully brought into being by the hand of the Creator. But in Kabbalah, the desire for healing the relationship between God and humanity as the benchmark heralding the Messiah's coming is expressly spoken, speaking what is not spoken about in the Torah.

And in the sefirot is a map toward God's knowledge, through the Divine attributes that most eloquently express God's nature. Remote and concealed, while revealed in a diverse Creation, God is served by the communicative aides, the sefirot, drawing closer to the seeking human soul with a sincere invitation to know God through these emanations.

While here as communicative emanations of the Divine, the sefirot collaborate with Creation, born in every moment. As the Baal Shem Tov (founder of Hasidism, 1698 - 1760), remarked on the concept of Continuous Creation (basing his comments on Psalms 33: 6), "...the

Ten Utterances used to create the world continue to stand, constantly re-creating the world" (Tanya, Shaar Hayichud Veha'emunah, c1). And it must be reborn in every moment to be healed finally, in the cosmology of the Sefer Yetzirah.

Etz Chaim – The Tree of Life

Organized in the form of a tree, the icon of the 10 sefirot incarnates God's attributes as a metaphysical source of life. Just as that tree "stood in the midst of the Garden of Eden" of Torah's Genesis Creation narrative, it continues to stand. Eternally bearing the fruit of the Divine, the tree is as creaturely as the humans who eat from it.

But what the tree stewards on behalf of its Creator is what that lofty Presence wants humanity to "know." What does God mean? What does God do? What is God trying to prove with this Creation business? All these questions may, at least partially, be answered by the fruit of Etz Chaim – the sefirot.

But its fruit is not easily plucked. It is approached, studied, consumed, digested, and transformed into the illumination of what the sefirot and the tree that bears it means.

Let's discover what the sefirot are named and what those names mean.

- **Keter** (Crown)
- **Chokhmah** (Wisdom)
- **Binah** (Understanding)
- **Chesed** (Lovingkindness)
- **Gevurah** (Might)
- **Tiferet** (Beauty)
- **Hod** (Splendor)
- **Netzah** (Victory)
- **Yesod** (Foundation)

- **Shekhinah** (Divine Presence), also called **Malkhut** (Sovereignty). NB: Shekhinah is a unique emanation, sited at the base of the Tree and thus, its root.

While an individual in the description, the sefirot form a system or network of mutual dependence. Borne within each sefirah are the other nine, expressing the integrity and unitive oneness of God. They work with and for each other, for humanity, and for Creation as a whole, on the part of the Divine.

For example, with beauty comes might (judgment), as tension is the nature of the Created Order. God has created opposites to support the "shape" of the whole energetically and the intention in which it was created.

But in the organization of the sefirot, we see God acting not from omnipotence but from a desire to educate. But why? What happened that might have compelled the Divine to so organizing an expository model to communicate the Divine Attributes when God's omnipotence might have found a more efficient means of doing so?

In the soul of the Torah, nothing is simple. Nothing is straightforward. But everything is attainable by understanding the framework of Etz Chaim as a gift. Creation is a gift, and so the sefirot provide the 10 clues we most desperately need to figure out how to heal it.

On that note, let's look at the Tree of Life as a model of the balance and symmetry of Creation itself.

Balance and Symmetry

Yetzer ha tov and *yetzer ha rah* are, respectively, the urge to the good and the urge to the evil. And just as the Tree of Life expressed homeostasis (balance) in Creation, the presence of good and evil in every human represents psychological homeostasis.

So, the question is, why is there evil in the world if, after having created the universe, God gazed upon the completed project and said it was "very good." That's an unequivocal statement, so apparently, it's as good as anything else in Creation is. But right after we talk about balance, we'll be talking about the Kabbalistic format of Creation, which explains the presence of the yetzer ha rah in the Created Order. The fact is, it's among us and in us, and as we read in Isaiah 45:7, God warned us thusly, "I form light and create darkness, I make weal and create woe; I the LORD do all these things."

But as discussed earlier, tension maintains the shape of Creation. Absent that tension, the Created Order ceases to exist. Imagine a world in which no one had the slightest ambition or desire to build a life. In the existence of both the evil and the good urge, we find the balance of life. We are neither all dark nor all light because we're part of a tainted and illusory Created Order. And that tension also exists in the balance and symmetry of the Etz Chaim. The sefirot on the right of the tree emanate traits expressing the unlimited goodness of God – Chokhmah (Wisdom), Chesed (Living kindness), and Netzah (Victory). Standing opposite these attributes are Binah (Understanding), Gevurah (Might), and Hod (Splendor), all speaking to the fearsome aspects of an omnipotent God.

In the center of the tree is Tiferet (Beauty), uniting the two sides. It's here that the sefirot are synthesized, representing the ideal balance of Creation. On the right side of the Tree, Chesed defines the other attributes in the column, while on the left, Gevurah (also referred to in some versions of the Tree as Din or Judgment) defines its column, expressing fearsome, awe-inspiring omnipotence. These two definitive sefirot explain the necessity of justice dispensed with mercy. Without mercy, justice would be a bludgeon that would smash Creation. Without justice, mercy's loveliest would simply melt it.

At the root of the Tree is Yesod (Foundation). This sefirah provides stability. But beneath it, in the earth itself, is Shekhinah/Malkhut (Divine Presence/Sovereignty). Standing apart but still interdependent with the others in the Tree, the Divine Presence/Sovereignty is the contact point between the Divine and humanity.

It's in the sefirot that the ineffable Divine's true nature is revealed. Through their agency, humanity is given the means to approach that unknowable God by understanding God's attributes, emanated by these witnesses to the Divine's concealed truth. They exist in the Creation model of the Sefer Yetzirah as teachers and guides, working to heal a primordial wound.

But before we get into the meat and potatoes of the matter, let's talk about the source document for the sefirot, Sefer ha Bahir (the Book of Brilliance). This First Century collection of wisdom is closely related to Sefer Yetzirah.

The Source Text

In the Sefer Yetzirah, we find further elaboration on the activity of the sefirot in Creation. But the acknowledged source of the sefirot, arranged as an icon of the Tree of Life, is the Sefer ha Bahir. The most acknowledged timing by secular scholars for the book's production is to the early 13th Century, attributing multiple authors. But it's regularly attributed to the 1st Century anonymous author or to Nehunya ben HaKanah (unknown). Nachmanides (1194 - 1270 CE) is said to be one of the first to attribute the work to HaKanah, calling it Midrash R. Nehunya ben HaKanah in the opening sentence to his commentary on Torah, discussing Genesis 1.

Named for its first narrative (and interpretation of Job 37:21, "Now, no one can look on the light when it is bright in the skies when the wind has passed and clear them"), the subject of the title might also be translated "illumination." Of course, the bright light in question is that of God, but the "brilliance" is also an allusion to the work in Creation of the sefirot, that is to act as the emissaries and emanations of God's principal traits.

While considered a foundational text of Kabbalah, Sefer ha Bahir is not really a book at all. It is a collection of parables that guide the reader to an understanding of the sefirot. With Sefer Yetzirah, Sefer ha Bahir became a primary text for developing Jewish Mysticism through time, with its contents redacted, glossed, and edited as it was pored over by generations of students, seeking the numinous.

In reality, a conglomeration of fragments of text, some ending in mid-sentence, Sefer ha-Bahir's most valuable contribution to Kabbalah has been that of the sefirot and pointing to their presence in Jewish thought throughout history. While this may or not be the case, given controversy regarding dating, the value of claiming such an early presence certainly lends weight to the mystical presence of the sefirot in even traditional Judaism and to the respect with which the Sefer Yetzirah is regarded. But in the end, it's the value of what's said in Sefer ha Bahir that's of primary importance – not the integrity of the physical text.

A Road Map to Creation

Sefer ha Bahir takes the format of a discussion involving the teacher and his students and is divided into 66 brief paragraphs, with 140 parables. Intended as an exegetical interpretation of the Creation narrative in Genesis, it goes beneath the text of Genesis to apply a mystical etiology, the question of "why things are the way they are." It also interprets the meaning of the shapes of Hebrew letters and their accompanying vowel points and cantillation symbols (markings which indicate emphasis when sung).

The book includes parables that act as miniature commentaries on specific verses in the Genesis narrative. Broken into 5 sections, the parables aren't strictly on-topic but seem to stay within the parameters of the themes at hand, with the sections:

I. Commentary on the Creation narrative of Genesis

II. A discussion of the Hebrew aleph-bet as the mystical stuff of Creation

III. The seven voices and the Sefirot

IV. The 10 Sefirot

V. Mysteries of the Soul and summation

It's in the Sefer ha Bahir that we read of the sefirot as emanations of God's attributes. While the Sefer Yetzirah describes in strikingly different terms (numerically, particularly), the goal is the same – to convey their purpose as emissaries of the concealed Divine. Which brings us to the question - "Why is God concealed?"

In the next section, we'll start at the very beginning of things, from the Kabbalistic standpoint. In doing so, we'll go back to the "formless void" of the Creation narrative of Genesis to discover what happened there, according to the Kabbalah.

In the Beginning

So, in the very act of Creation, the Divine Creator chose to be concealed? That seems strange until you read the Kabbalistic interpretation and explanation for the Creation of the universe and its purpose.

The subject is dense and rich, so in an effort not to overwhelm readers, I will break our discussion into sections. Now that we've discussed the basics, let's move on to the nuts and bolts of the Kabbalistic model of Creation, in the concepts of tzimtzum, shevirah, reshimu, and tikkun. Let's read about what the Kabbalists found when they scratched the surface of the Genesis Creation narrative.

Chapter Four: The Sefirot II - Becoming Something

One of the Kabbalistic literature goals is to find the way forward to a healed relationship between God and humanity. That's the desired outcome. But before the outcome can be desired, the story of the Genesis Creation narrative must be understood in mystical terms.

The terms form a spectacular story of Creation's foundation, which are the seeds of its ultimate destruction.

Let's read the story of Creation from the Kabbalistic perspective in its concepts and assertions about the sefirot and how they came to be.

A Formless Void

"In the beginning, when God created the heavens and the earth, the earth was a formless void and darkness covered the face of the deep, while a wind from God swept over the face of the waters." Genesis 1: 1 - 2

The evocative first lines of the Book of Genesis describe the universe as a "formless void." When we think of a formless void, the assumption is that its substance is not significant in any real way. We assume that there is "nothing." In Hebrew, the formless void is "tohu wa-bohu." The expression is found also in Isaiah 34:11, translated in the NRSV as "primordial chaos."

While the word "tohu" is employed with frequency in the Book of Isaiah to men's "vanity," the word "bohu" is only found in 3 instances – Genesis 1: 2a, Isaiah 23: 11, as described above, and in Jeremiah 4:23 (translated in NRSV as "waste and void"). Scholars believe this to be "paronomasia," that is the use of a rhyming word and is a type of pun. But this seems somewhat dismissive of the Hebrew text.

The Septuagint (the Hellenistic or Greek translation of the Hebrew Scriptures) applies a more profound meaning to the expression, especially after revisions applied to the text by Aquila, Theodotion, and Symmachus. Projecting the hypotheses reached by Greek philosophy, the early commentators on the Septuagint (whether Jewish, Christian, or Greek) concluded that tohu wa bohu could be interpreted to mean matter in a primordial state of chaos (as interpreted in the NRSV, above).

As Parmenides (5th Century BCE), the father of Greek philosophical cosmology, expounded, "ex nihilo nihil fit" (nothing comes from nothing). In this vein, the writers and redactors of the Septuagint followed, bearing a heavy influence on the sages of Kabbalah.

So, while the world of the Genesis Creation narrative is a "formless void," that void is not immaterial. That void holds within it the potential of being the raw material for Creation, which arrives in the Divine intellect as almost a spark of instinctual knowledge – inspiration.

In the model of Kabbalah, the "formless void/primordial chaos" is a starting point. In its presumed nothingness is something which has not yet become. It awaits the breath of the Creator to form and define it, just as God animated the mud doll in Genesis 2: 7, which reads, "Then the LORD God formed man from the dust of the ground and breathed into his nostrils the breath of life, and the man became a living being."

Tohu wa-bohu is not about nothingness. As explained by the sages, the expression conveys that primordial chaos demands an ordering hand/breath to actuate its potential. But to do this, space must be made.

Ayin (I am Becoming)

In defining the status of the nascent Created Order before the intervention of the Divine, tohu wa bohu is joined by "ayin" (meaning, I am becoming).

What's implied by the meaning of the word is a "nothing," that is becoming "something." Like primordial chaos, Ayin is not the presumed state of "nothingness." Rather, it's a state of something coming into being.

Sited in the Hebrew language in close relation to "yesh" (something, being, existence), the state of Ayin is primordial, existing in the "formless void" (or perhaps is that formless void, itself). But somehow, Ayin became a dwelling place for the Divine in which the Creative spark might be ignited.

And that spark is the Ohr Ein Sof (the endless light), which reaches beyond all boundaries and limitations which might contain it. Like a ray of the sun, the Ohr Ein Sof is the product of its source, discernable as the result of the fiery holistic radiance emanating it. And in its missionary beauty, it hints at the fullness of the Divine. The light of God is what a Christian might call it, but the Kabbalistic interpretation of this light and its first manifestation in Ayin is metaphysical poetry, which casts God as First Mover. In that role, the Divine Builder first lights a candle to investigate the creative urge, which has arrived in the celestial precincts as Divine instinct, the inspiration.

While transcending the sefirot, Ohr Ein Sof is intrinsic to their existence and the reason for it. This duality follows the integrity of Divinity and its eternality, as laid out repeatedly in Hebrew Scripture. Because God's inner workings and total reality are beyond all comprehension, what God does to facilitate the healing of the Divine/human relationship is God's business. And if God is so inclined to send the residual light of God's glory into Creation as a sub-contractor in the project of building it, that doesn't represent a breaching of the Oneness of God. It represents something much more like "multitasking."

For this reason, the primordial chaos/formless void/tohu wa bohu of Ayin is intimately associated with Ein Sof (the limitless, the omnipotent, the endless, the ineffable). Ein Sof is, in essence, the Creative force in the universe or the primordial version of the One God (being similarly without limits and existing in inviolable unity).

And here, we must pause to recognize the word "yesh" and its relationship to the Kabbalistic Creation narrative.

Yesh Café?

The modern Hebrew expression that serves at the heading for this section means "Is there coffee?"

But once upon a time, the word "yesh" meant something else in Hebrew, and in terms of Torah/Talmud/Kabbalah, it continues to take the classical meaning. All the same, it's not a waste of time to ask about the implications of the meaning this word has taken on in modern, spoken Hebrew.

As we've read above, the Hebrew word "yesh" means "something/being/existence." This is the simple evolution of the modern Hebrew, "Is there coffee?" But there is a deeper meaning.

That meaning lies in the question, "Is there?" This is the question asked by yesh. If yesh is, indeed, something/being/existence, then perhaps the fullness of the question is something like "is there something/being/existence." Because "yesh" is as much a question as a manifestation of ontology (on the nature of being).

As there is, globally, in Hebrew philosophy and theology, there's a basis in the questions asked by the juxtaposition of the two words "Ayin" and "yesh," which suggests a tension. But the relationship between the two words is much more than that. It suggests a primordial chaos/formless void, raw material awaiting the molding hand/breath of the Creator.

This brings us to the concepts of Yesh me-Ayin (something created from nothing) and **Ayin me-Yesh** (nothing created from something). These point to the insignificance of attempting to define the substance or lack thereof, suggested by either; a God is the only genuine reality extant in Creation.

In summary, Creation is an illusion, suggested by the provocative dance between Yesh and Ayin. In the end, "yesh ma yesh" (potential/raw material that is becoming something) is the suggestively vague and yet sufficiently mystical answer to the question. The interpretations which attach to these ideas and the philosophical assertions underpinning them have occupied Kabbalists for generations, bringing us the spectacularly analytical spiritual philosophy of Kabbalah.

"Yesh café? (Is there coffee?)" That's a hopeful question. But "Yesh Bereishit? (Is there Creation?)– that's a metaphysical question that implies neither hope nor despair, and in that question, it reflects the exploratory nature of Kabbalah and the Sefer Yetzirah itself. While clear that the trajectory of Sefer Yetzirah and other Kabbalistic literature diverges from an "ex nihilo" Creation model, students must follow the yellow brick road to draw the conclusion for themselves.

But how does all this concern the concealment of the primordial Creator?

Igniting Creation

In Ayin, the Creator finds the creative spark, resulting in the manifestation of the Limitless Light there. This is the work of the sefirah Keter (Crown), also called "Keter Elyon" (the Crown of the Most High). At the top of the sefirot in Etz Chaim, the Keter works to herald God's rising to the creative spark. This spark occurs in the instinct, preceding the cognitive act of confronting what that spark is referring to – in other words, thought.

Keter stands as an emblem of Ein Sof and the crowning of students of Kabbalah upon the death of their egos in achievement union with God.

But the name of God, Keter Elyon, also appears in Torah, in the narrative of the burning bush (Exodus 3: 1 – 21). In verse 13, Moses asks to know God's name to return to his exiled people in Egypt with a sign of God's favor.

And God responds, "Ehyeh asher ehyeh" ("I will be what I will be" or "I am That I am That.") This is the locus classicus of the Tetragrammaton, in its y-h-v-h (yed, hey, vav, hey) composition, which implies a similar unwillingness to share secret plans and attendant motives with the Prophet or anyone else. The implication is that the truth of God is to be sought, *not revealed promiscuously.*

In naming himself as "Ehyeh," God tells Moses that a name cannot hope to contain the limitless. In fact, naming is an act of power that imposes the will of another, and so, God implicitly tells Moses that's it none of his business. The Ineffable will not be asked – and certainly will not answer – such questions.

It's in that spirit – of Divine unknowability and sovereign primacy – that the sefirah of Keter expresses itself. It is not a material crown. Rather, it's an emblem of the pursuit of the spark in knowledge on the human level. On the level of the Divine, it stands as a symbol of humanity seeking repair of its relationship with God.

But beyond the Primordial God's presence in Ayin, what else is going on there?

Making Space – Tzimtzum

In the potentiality offered by Ayin (nothing that's becoming something – or potential, which is already "something"), God is concealed as an integral part of the creative process. This is a Divine strategy, in which God makes space in the realm of potential, becoming its "activator."

The father of Lurianic Kabbalah, Isaac Luria, saw tzimtzum as a sudden event. As the Primordial God, Ein Sof contracted into a space just beyond the Created Order. In doing so, the "limitless" became "limited."

Translated directly from Hebrew, "tzimtzum" is rendered as "contraction." But inherent to that contraction is transformation. Chaim Vital (1543 - 1620), the author of the text, Etz Chaim, explains in that volume that Ohr Ein Sof (light of the limitless) while manifesting the Divine, does so ethereally by taking on the properties of creaturely light. Impermanent, the light of Ohr Ein Sof similarly reduced itself to model the properties of the created version of itself to conceal itself, as Ein Soft had. Transformed into a lesser version of itself, it hides in plain sight.

You can't stare directly into the sun, but you can enjoy its warmth and its diffused light, which is the purpose of the Light of the Limitless.

So, to make the requisite space for Creation, God's first instinct became a plan taking shaping in the concealing potentiality that is Ayin. And as that plan took shape, Ein Sof made space to accommodate those plans by limiting its limitlessness.

Concealed and Emanating

What's important to understand here is that Ein Sof did more than contract and conceal in tzimtzum. God also transformed the true nature of the Divine to accommodate the plan of Creation. More than that, God, is so transforming, created a means by which it was possible to emanate the Divine traits, infusing the Created Order with them and guiding humanity back into communion, by so doing.

Key to apprehending the Kabbalistic Creation narrative is remembering the immutable unity of the One God. That unity is not only immutable; it is ineffable and thus, may "be what it will be." In the Book of Malachi, it's written, "I, God, do not change" (Malachi 3:6). In this instance, transformation is not so much alteration as a clever hiding place and an even cleverer disguise. Ein Sof does what is deemed most expedient while remaining the creative and ordering force of the universe.

And so, both immanent and detached, Ein Sof begins the work of Creation by withdrawing from it, so huge that the contraction represented by tzimtzum is necessary. But to reveal Divine Power, Ein Sof creates the universe, manifesting in the Created Order through Ohr Ein Sofi and the sefirot's disguised agency.

This means there is space for free will in the relationship between Ein Sof and his human creations. With the contraction of the Divine in tzimtzum, God grants the human-animal the space to discover Ein Sof. Concealed and yet immanent, God invites humanity for a game of hiding and seek. In this model, accepting the invitation is the first step on the journey of 1,000 miles toward reunification with the source of our very existence.

Were God not to so conceal himself, instead preferring omnipotence and the non-negotiable imposition of the Divine Will, humanity could not aspire to the spiritual revelation of any kind, not having a truly free will to operate within.

Shevirot ha Kelim (The Breaking of the Vessels) – Shevirah

The concept of Shevirah derives from the work of Isaac Luria in 1570. Called "shevirat ha kelim" (the breaking of the vessels), the 10 sefirot are represented as simple containers. Unable to continue containing the Ohr Ein Sof, they shatter, and in this shattering, Creation is instigated. Drawing his conclusions from studying Zohar, his later work forms the interpretative framework used by all Kabbalists after 1570 in interpreting the work of the sefirot and what they mean, as depicted in Sefer ha Bahir and Sefer Yetzirah.

The vessels' cataclysmic shattering takes place in the "formless void" of "primordial chaos" – tohu. And when they shatter, their contents are spilled throughout creation, but the shards are also scattered.

The shards, the outer means of containment, are called the kelipot (singular: kelipah). In their shattering, the Ohr Ein Sof is released into the created order, but these shards accompany them, and that's a very salient point in the model of balance through tension the Kabbalists were seeking to underline.

Occurring in the realm of chaos, the form of the kelipot stands as the primordial form of the sefirot, before their state of interdependence, in the format of Etz Chaim. That primordial format is "shattered" in shevirah.

While the shattering of the vessels bestows the Holiness of the God's Light on Creation, the origin of the physical container is sitra achra (evil; the other side). Like nutshells, these must be cracked to release the nut within. This metaphor reveals the truth - that even contained within evil, the Light of God busts out.

In the shattering of the vessels is also the lesson of free will. Humanity is not given a free ride in a world devoid of spiritual peril. Rather, humanity chooses to seek God in that brilliant light or to content itself with the broken shards of kelipot in seeking and doing evil.

As the kelipot shatter, nitzotzot (Holy Sparks) are released. These sparks of Ohr Ein Sof may be found and ignited through the performance of the mitzvot, in response to the origin of the kelipot in sitra achra. But the choice is ours to make.

The word "shevirah" is from the Hebrew word "shever," meaning "broken." This word crops up repeatedly in Judaism and its theme of brokenness and wholeness in Creation's constituent parts and in human life. For example, at the conclusion of a Jewish wedding ceremony, a glass is wrapped in cloth and stomped on by the groom, after which the congregation affirms, "L'Chaim!" (to life). The Seder starts with the breaking of whole matzah (unleavened bread). In the sounding of the shofar (ceremonial ram's horn, which is blown through to produce a sound), we hear brokenness. All these symbolic actions represent the brokenness of human life, poignantly expressed in Jewish history and in the narratives of the Bible.

In the breaking of the matzah lives the story of slavery in Egypt and the brokenness of the slave. In the notes sounded by the shofar, we hear the shevirah and the regret embodied when we bow before the Creator in repentance. And in breaking the glass following a wedding, we remember the destruction of the Temple as a wound in search of healing, eternally.

Speaking to Jewish History

The sweeping narrative of the Creation of the universe in the shattering of the vessels also has a parallel theme, speaking directly to Jewish History. This begins in the Biblical narrative of Moses at Mt. Sinai and continues in the destruction of the two Temples. But the theme of shattering and the reality of God in the darkest places Creation offers is continued throughout the history of the Jewish People, in the brutality of events like the Crusades and other profoundly traumatic and shattering events.

There is a profound clue to the nature of the shevirah event in Isaiah 45: 7, which reads, "I form the light and create darkness; I make peace and create evil. I, the LORD, do all these things". This single verse is the basis for the Kabbalistic interpretation of shevirah as the origin of free will and the basis for the existence of evil in God's "very good" Creation.

In Exodus 32: 1 – 20, Moses has ascended to Mt. Sinai, leaving the People to their own devices, and those devices was idolatrous. With the Prophet's back turned, they'd produced a "calf of gold." Given a "heads up" by God, Moses returns to the Israelites and, seeing the calf, smashes the tablets that bear the received commandments on the ground.

With the second set bestowed by God later in Exodus 34:28, these broken tablets were placed in the Ark of the Covenant. Broken, they are not useless. They are instructive, and they are part of the story of God's presence among the Israelites. In brokenness, they continue to speak of God's place in the lives of the people and the consequences for "breaking" that relationship. Placed in the Ark with the second set of whole tablets, they also served as a symbol of hope and of ongoing repair of the relationship between humanity and the Divine. Good and evil – wholeness and brokenness – are present in the chambers of the human heart as they were once in the Ark of the Covenant, as it made its way to the Promised Land and in the company of the Israelites.

Both the Kabbalistic Creation narrative, in shevirah and the Exodus narrative of the shattering of the 10 Commandments remind us that life is difficult. It comes with both brokenness and wholeness, and that both these estates must be honored as being equally important to the living of human lives. Even harbored in the Holy of Holies, the most Holy of all places in God's Creation, our brokenness and wholeness exist as part of the greater Order.

We all are defined as much by our scars as we are by our triumphs in life. And the shevirah reminds us that even Creation was forged in brokenness, only made whole by the presence of God's Light and its continual apprehension by humanity. Evil is as eternal as God, having been Created as part of the whole's reality. But in our response to evil is our truest humanity, provoked by a question to draw near to the Ohr Ein Sof, once contained in the kelipot.

The goodness of Creation is balanced by the evil released into it by those shards. In the same way, the brokenness of the original 10 Commandments is balanced by the wholeness of the second set of the tablets, borne with the Israelites in the Ark, ever pursued by the Divine Presence, Shekhinah.

Right in the Exodus narrative is the theme of shevirah and that of tikkun. In a just Creation wrought by the word of a loving God, the broken is redeemed when we seek that restoration, bearing our brokenness with our wholeness in deference to the truth. That wholeness without brokenness is an unbalanced and thus, a deficient state in a balanced Created Order held together in Divine tension.

Reshimu

Best translated as "residue." After the tzimtzum and the breaking of the vessels, there remained the "letters of the residue." Like the residue clinging to the inside of an empty olive oil bottle, reshimu is a reminder, describing the self-limitation of God in tzimtzum, but also referring to the residue of Ohr Ein Sof as seen in the created order as a "limited" or creaturely version of itself.

Reshimu is what provides the definition, using the vehicle of language. With the letters of the aleph-bet constructing meaning, they stand as "kelim." The characters, themselves, convey meaning, bearing within them the Divine Light.

The work of the Kelim was initiated in the tzimtzum. Bearing within them the Orh Ein Sof, they were assigned as agents of definition, representing the potential of the concealment/contraction of the Divine for the sake of the Created Order. Subsequently drained of that Divine Light, they facilitate the limitation of the limitless by creating boundaries.

Another way to think of reshimu is "memory." Our human memories encompass our life stories, and while we can return to what we remember to visit it, we can't live those stories again, except in our minds. We remember flavors. We remember scents. These, in turn, remind us of life events. Our memories and the residual taste in our mouths and scents in our nostrils, long after their direct experience, are analogous to the traces of the Limitless One we draw near in Kabbalah.

Reshimu is a residue found in Creation which links directly to the concealed God, and again, it stands as a clue and an invitation.

Tikkun

Tikkun olam (repair of the world) has, with the rise of interest in Kabbalah in recent times, taken on a meaning completely different from the original intent of the Lurianic/Kabbalistic model of Creation. In that model, the repair intended is spiritual, which the popular conception interprets to mean healing the world on a physical level through activism and acts of kindness. While these are noble and necessary pursuits, they are not the tikkun olam intended in the model we're discussing.

Luria's intent was the reestablishment of the relationship between God and humanity via the reconstruction of the kelim by way of the mitzvot and, of course, an intense study of Torah. The Hasidic Jewish community is the leading proponent of the Lurianic viewpoint, which seeks the Divine Presence through daily acts that might otherwise be deemed mundane. But even brushing your teeth is sanctified in Hasidic practice, in the satisfaction of the 613 mitzvot, covering everything from food and the other detritus of daily life to worship and appropriate punishment for misdeeds. The mitzvot stand as "reparative" actions that follow God's will. In these, the Hasidim define their path toward tikkun by scrupulously following the mitzvot in every aspect of their lives.

Luria's Tikkun

The process of tikkun in Isaac Luria's model of Creation, followed by the Hasidim, is spirituality materialized. This runs parallel to the popular conception of tikkun as physical actions that add to the restoration of material Creation. The spiritual model similarly posits repair through action, but these actions are strictly defined by halakhah (Jewish Law) as received by Moses at Sinai.

Isaac Luria believed that the work of tikkun was achieved in creating Adam – Primordial Man. But his conception of Adam Kadmon was Adam's figure as a spiritual being of light and the direct conduit of that light.

Adam Kadmon is also the First of the Worlds to be formed, following the Divine's tzimtzum/concealment, representing existence itself (the Four Worlds will be discussed shortly). While not yet the Created Order, the world is a Divine thought.

In addition, Adam, with the means to achieve tikkun, having received instruction from the Divine in the Divine breath (ruach) that animated him, was thus positioned to "pick up the pieces" (those shattered vessels). He was the point person for the true plan of

Creation, living in the Garden – its most vibrant expression. He had Eve. He had everything he needed to satisfy the Divine Will.

And yet, Adam didn't follow the plan. Instead, he reached up, took hold of the apple Eve offered him, and took a bite. With just one lousy bite, a genuine monkey wrench had been thrown into the Creator's scheme. And with that bite, at that very moment, all the work that tikkun had wrought in God's service was undone.

This interpretation of the shevirah posits that shevirah occurred to purify the Divine of evil. The Ohr Ein Sof, transmuted and in a clever disguise, could no longer be so purified, as Adam had been a crucial part of the setup. Because of Adam's preference for satisfying his own personal appetites over those of the Creator, he broke faith with God, having not absorbed the lessons intended for him. Had he done so; he never would have reached for that apple.

So, even with Primordial Man being animated by the breath of the Divine, the creature's physicality wins, with its childlike needs and demands. Cleaving to the physical world with such ferocity he knocks over the whole creative apple cart, Adam's acceptance of the apple is how evil came to infect Creation, just as surely as any virus, due to the breaking of the vessels in shevirah.

But before we move on, let's acquaint ourselves with the Four Worlds (starting with Adam Kadmon) and how they figure in the realm of the sefirot.

The Four Worlds and a Fifth

The sefirot's complex world is endless, and the Four Worlds is just one more mystical window on the complex workings of the Divine from the Kabbalistic standpoint.

Adam Kadmon could not have been the world in which Creation was established due to its proximity to its source, created from the Divine's original contraction in tzimtzum. Because of the nearness of the Ohr Ein Sof source, it required a filtration system to better disguise itself. This fifth world, too divinely sublime and ideal to even be perceived, stands as a symbol of God's transcendent will.

Emanating from the Adam Kadmon, the light manifests as disparate beams, experienced in the cosmos as energy. In Hebrew, this is called "ha einayim" (light shining forth from the eyes), and the eyes these beams are emanating from are those of Adam Kadmon. These beams number 10.

They serve as a metaphor, describing the descent from an essential level (level of the essence of things) to a sensory level, or the phenomenological plane (physical phenomena). In Kabbalistic terms, the beams of light are potent, as they descend as manifestations of Keter/Crown, signifying their source but never revealing it fully. These are the primordial sefirot, revealing themselves embodiments of their primordial realm - tohu – the "formless void/primordial chaos.

The Primordial Sefirot

In their realized form (as you're thinking of them while you read this book), the 10 sefirot contain the elements or attributes of the others. They contain worlds within their one emanative world.

But in their primordial form in the realm of tohu, the sefirot don't exist as we understand them today. In this chaotic stew of matter sitting around idle, the sefirot exist in isolation. They do not interact or even so much as know about each other.

Beaming from the "eyes" of Adam Kadmon, though, they take on the disguised light of Ohr Ein Sof, each becoming a manifestation of it. And because of the lack of teamwork among the primordial sefirot, they cannot contain the light, causing the shattering. In this explanation of the primordial sefirot and their shattering, they cannot contain the Divine light, being undeveloped and thus, poorly adapted to the requirements.

Having ruled in isolation, the sefirot shatter, each dying in turn.

While a catastrophe, it's a catastrophe with a distinct purpose, though. As we've seen above, shevirah also breaks the light up into manageable sections, each reflecting an attribute of its Divine source. So, the shevirah is not only responsible for distributing evil into Creation (as a balance to good) but for Creation's very diversity.

To unite Creation in that diversity, though, tikkun is the answer. In Hebrew, this word means "restitution, "reclamation," or "reformation." And this is tikkun's most specific mission – to gather in the shattered pieces of the sefirot of tohu, reordering Creation in its intended form.

And it's in the Four Worlds that the sefirot we've come to know (or are just acquainting ourselves with) were crystallized from the stuff of the formless void. Let's review the Four Worlds to get a feeling for how they connect with the 10 sefirot in our next chapter – Part III of the Sefirot.

Chapter Five: The Sefirot III – Becoming Creation

Now that we've met primordial Man, Adam Kadmon, it's clear that Isaac Luria's concept of humanity was high. His interpretation of earlier works in the canon of Kabbalah (Sefer Yetzirah and Sefer ha Bahir) takes on a highly complex and technical model, rooted in spirituality. But his placement of Adam Kadmon as a fifth world; an idealized version of fallen humanity, through which the Ohr Ein Sof emanates into Creation through the Four Worlds, represents a model of humanity which sits so near the Throne of God as to be almost unthinkable.

But that's where Adam Kadmon is, casting the light from his eyes downward to the formative sefirot, animating the emanative attributes of God with the filtered Light of the Divine.

From there, the descent of the concealed God begins through the four-stage model of Lurianic Creation – the Four Worlds. These names of these Worlds are found in a single verse in the Bible, Isaiah 43: 7, which reads, "Every one that is called by My name and for My **glory** (Atzilut "Emanation/Close"), I have **created** (Beriah "Creation"), I have **formed** (Yetzirah "Formation"), even I have **made** (Assiyah "Action").

Atzilut (Spirit)

Here is where the sefirot we know came to be manifested. The name of this world is from " aitzel," meaning "next to." Aitzel may also be translated as "emanating from." Atzilut comes into being as the first action of the Divine, in the tzimtzum/concealment. For this reason, this world remains in the precincts of the Most High. This world governs emanations and causes.

In this world, the sefirot take on their true purpose - to emanate the Divine attributes. In Atzilut, the sefirot take on their individual yet interdependent roles, each bearing within them the full scope of the Divine attributes. Through their agency, the concealed God is vicariously revealed in the manifestation of the Holy traits.

Chokhmah (wisdom) is the sefirah corresponding to Atzilut.

Beriah (Intellect)

In Beriah, the light descends from its source, through the eyes of Adam Kadmon. While not yet material, Creation is beginning to be discernable.

The word of this World expressly means "creation," so in this world, the creative process takes on a life of its own.

The World of Beriah is also called Kisei ha Kavod (Divine Throne). In this model, God has descended and is in contact with what's being made tangible in Beriah's processing unit.

Beriah is the locus in which souls and the Angels are created. The Seraphim (from the root seraphah – fire) acts as agents to satisfy Creation's energetic necessities, remaining in close contact with the Creator, carrying the Divine Passion's uncontainable fire as fuel.

The sefirah Binah corresponds to Beriah.

Yetzirah (Emotion)

Yetzirah is the Hebrew word, which is the name of Sefer Yetzirah. And as a World, it's where the final form of Creation is established. As the light descends through the Worlds, it begins to look like the finished product in Yetzirah.

This world is where the chayot ha kodesh (the holy beings) dwell, namely the archangels, Raphael, Gabriel, and Michael. Each corresponds to a sefirah, with Raphael corresponding to Tiferet, Gabriel to Gevurah, and Michael to Chesed. Each archangel operates in Yetzirah according to the trait corresponded to. Raphael operates within the realm of Beauty, Gabriel within that of Might, and Michael, within that of Lovingkindness.

With the sefirot, the archangels co-create, infusing Creation with the traits of the Divine, weaving them as threads throughout the Created Order.

The 6 emotional sefirot, from Chesed through Yesod, correspond to Yetzirah.

Assiyah (Action)

The name of this World means "action," and that's exactly what happens here. Having descended from the light emitted from the eyes of Adam Kadmon, descending through the previous three Worlds, the Divine spark of creative inspiration is now becoming the final form of Creation.

With the Divine imagination having flowed through the creative superhighways forged by the archangels in Yetzirah, in conjunction with their corresponding sefirot, the 4 kingdoms on earth are formed here – human, mineral, vegetable, and animal.

With God concealed from what is being wrought by an act of Divine Will, Creation does not know of its source. Without that knowledge, the intent of free will is underlined. Humanity, ignorant of the Creative Force, has no obligation to go looking for it. That's a matter of free will. We are invited. But we're under no obligation to

RSVP.

Assiyah stands as a challenge. In its final revelation of Creation is that challenge – to find the hiding place of the source of all that has been created and to ask the questions that stand as clues in pursuing the Divine mystery.

Associated with Shekhinah/Malkhut, the Divine Presence is the question asked of humanity. It is infused in every fiber of the Created Order, with the attributes emanated by its fellow sefirot. So, Ein Sof, hidden in the vacuum created for that purpose, is both immanent and distant. God's traits are held in the stuff of Creation, which reflects the Divine, in name, traits, and sovereignty.

In Assiyah is the final autonomy of Creation from its Creator. Removed from it and yet directly descended from Divine Light, humanity stands as its steward. Will this steward of Creation respond to the invitation to play "hide and seek" with the hidden God who has made all that is?

Spiritual Psychology and the Four Worlds

While we can see their function in the broader context of the Lurianic exposition on Kabbalah's model of Creation, the Four Worlds have a larger purpose in the life of Jewish Mysticism.

These Four Worlds continue to exist and inform human life, each corresponding (as noted above in the headings to each section) with the human spirit, intellect, emotion, and action. In the first three of the worlds, we find the realms of our internal lives. Connected directly to Adam Kadmon, the first of these worlds is Atzilut, the realm of the human spirit.

Rabbi Zalman Schachter-Salomi (1924 - 2014) is the founder of the Jewish Renewal movement (also called "Four Worlds Judaism." Born into a liberal Belzer Hasidic family in Poland, "Rav Zalman," as he's known, is today remembered as an innovator and champion of ecumenism (interfaith dialogue). Ordained a rabbi in the Chabad Lubavitch tradition, Rav Zalman left the Hasidic lifestyle in the early 1960s.

But his mission was to restore the spirituality of the Jewish Diaspora through the transformation of Hassidism. While leaving the existing tradition, Schachter-Salomi brought forward the Ashkenazi Hassidim's mysticism, as laid out in Kabbalah, universalizing it.

We'll follow his interpretation of the Four Worlds in human life here. Rav Zalman believed that all humans simultaneously inhabit all Four Worlds.

In Atzilut, the World most intimately connected to the Divine via Adam Kadmon, the spirituality and the essence of all things is encountered. As the world of emanation (of the Divine Light and the Divine inspiration), the human soul seeks the mystical wisdom lying beneath Torah's words and letters, with its inner soul, Kabbalah, as a guide.

Beriah is the World of the intellect, our human sentience and consciousness, and the unique human capacity for reason and thought. Here, the human mind interprets the words of the Torah through the expository tales of Midrash. In this World, God is continually creating, breathing/speaking Creation eternally, and in so doing, re-creating the human intellect to seek the Divine.

In the World of Yetzirah, human emotions and the capacity to connect to each other and to God are central. This is the World in which we read the Torah through the lens of our emotions. Our intellects formed and our spirits alive, our emotions now inform our reading, molding our hearts into the shape in which they're vulnerable to the work of God and ready to be spiritually completed.

Finally, we arrive at the World of Assiyah. In this World of Action, we synthesize our spirits, intellects, and emotions to become co-creators in the work of tikkun and apprehend Torah for its most straightforward interpretation. We actively seek God in this final World, doing what's required to reach toward the Divine source, so long concealed.

In the Four Worlds, the 4 means of interpreting Torah, as defined by Pardes (the acronym for these four methods), are found:

- Peshat – the straightforward, plain meaning of the text

- Remez – meaning "hints," this method seeks a symbolic or esoteric meaning

- Drash – meaning "inquiry," this is the midrashic (exegetical) meaning, by way of comparison with other Jewish religious texts

- Sod – the mystical meaning, received via revelation or inspiration

Looking at these four interpretive frameworks, it's not difficult to see how they correspond to the Four Worlds of AbiYah (the acronym to describe them collectively). Peshat corresponds to Assiyah (Action). Remez corresponds to Yetzirah (Spirit). Drash corresponds to Beriah (Intellect), and Sod corresponds to Atzilut (emotion).

In the descent of the Ohr Ein Sof, we see a distinct progression from an emotional reading of Torah to an intellectual, exegetical one, to a spiritual one to arrive at the most straightforward interpretation of Torah in the physical plane of Assiyah.

Above them, all is the secret world of primordial Man, the anthropomorphic "World" of Adam Kadmon, the icon of pre-Creation, and of the primordial Sefirot. This is the world of sod b'sh sod (secret within a secret). Adam Kadmon is considered the Divine source of Torah and all hidden wisdom held within it an ideal "yechidah" (meaning "unity," expressly between humanity and God), as revealed to (and ignored by) the physical Adam of the Garden.

In Kabbalistic thought, the 10 sefirot are how Creation is realized, through their agency and that of Adam Kadmon (the highest "World") and the Angels. The Four Worlds exist as a metaphysical reality, containing the progressive Creation on its way to becoming something; on its journey to being born as God's name and as God's revelation to humanity (while revealing only the attributes of God through the sefirot).

The study of sefirot is endless, as these emanations of the Divine attributes represent the Limitless, omnipotent God, as conceptualized in Sefer ha Bahir and Sefer Yetzirah, the two foundational texts of Kabbalah. Here, I hope I've been able to provide you with a worthy overview of their intended role and how they relate to the Creation narrative in the model advanced by Jewish Mysticism.

But there is so much more we need to discuss in this book, so now, I would like to turn your attention to a later development arising from Sefer Yetzirah and one of the most fascinating figures of the canon of Kabbalah – the golem.

Chapter Six: Please Don't Try This at Home – the Golem

Everyone knows Frankenstein. But not everyone knows that the Modern Prometheus unleashed on the world by Mary Shelley (1797 – 1851) in 1818 was based on two other mythical life forms – the Golem and the Ancient Greek figure of Prometheus.

So, let's start our journey into the Golem's Kabbalistic world with a visit to Ancient Greece to see how Prometheus fits in.

Playing with Fire

The first work of science fiction, Mary Shelley wrote her tale of man made by a man at 18. An incredible achievement, to be sure. But what's truly incredible about it is her understanding of the tale of Prometheus. When read through a Kabbalistic lens, this story resonates with humanity's prohibition tampering with God's plans as detailed in the religious texts of Judaism.

Prometheus, the most intelligent of all the Titans of Greek mythology, made a terrible tactical error when he stole fire and gave it to humans to use for their own devices. In much the same way that Adam ate of the fruit of the Tree of the Knowledge of Good and Evil,

Prometheus transgressed the boundaries of his context. For the gods had declared that the power of fire was to be reserved to their use only, lest humanity believes itself to be equal to them.

And the punishment for Prometheus' transgression was macabre. Zeus declared that he should be chained to a rock on a mountain where he would be condemned to having his liver eaten – eternally. Each day, an eagle would find Prometheus, chained, and eat his liver. The story recounts that Prometheus' liver would regenerate each night to be ready for the eagle to eat it yet again the next morning. Like a hideous, Ancient Greek version of "Groundhog Day," this was to be the fate of the Titan who played with fire against the wishes of the gods.

Finally freed by Heracles (with Zeus's permission), Prometheus sheds his chains, repenting of his foolish action.

In Prometheus's tale, we see an Ancient Greek version of the Creation story, especially from a Kabbalistic standpoint. The Adam of the Genesis Creation narrative is similarly disobedient, transgressing the boundaries of the Created Order by eating the forbidden fruit of the Tree, which imparts all knowledge -specifically for God's use. But why wouldn't it be helpful for the first humans to eat the fruit of this tree? Why was it forbidden? Genesis 3: 5 explains this, reading, "For God knows that when you eat it, your eyes will be opened, and you will be like God, knowing good and evil."

So, Zeus wanted to keep the fire from humanity, and the God of the Bible wanted to keep the knowledge of good and evil from humanity. In verse is the reason, and it's precisely the same reason that Prometheus was punished for playing with fire – humans cannot approach the level of the godhead due to their creaturely status.

It's helpful to understand the meaning of the "Knowledge of good and evil" in the Ancient Near East and what it meant to people living in that time. Basically, it meant "the knowledge of everything." In other words, Prometheus' great error was to elevate humanity to the level of the gods of Mount Olympus by providing them with fire, and Adam's was the same. Omniscience is not a trait to which creaturely humans may aspire. Omniscience is for the gods (or the God of the Bible) alone.

Merism was a literary device employed often in the Ancient Near East, presenting two equivalent statements that represent opposites. In this book, we've been reading about balance in the Created Order, expressed through the sefirotic tree and other semiotic and literary devices, so merism is a type of rhetorical balance used to express a total concept not juxtaposing (comparing) but by synthesizing opposing forces.

In the Hebrew Scriptures, merisms are employed liberally, for instance, in Genesis 1:1, in which God creates "the heavens and the earth." These two apparently opposing realities (see the Four Worlds, in which the Created Order is located as far away from the concealed God as possible) are expressive of a totality that reaches beyond them. What is intended is to encompass the whole of Creation, as expressed in two apparently opposite realities. This is also seen in Genesis 1: 5. In this verse, "morning" and "evening" mean one 24-hour day.

Likewise, "the knowledge of good and evil" in the Ancient World intended "the knowledge of everything there is to know." And so, by pretending to the omniscience of God, Adam erred (in an epic fashion, having derailed tikkun olam), and Prometheus erred by offering the advantages of Mount Olympus to mere mortals.

Mary Shelley's Frankenstein

In casting Dr. Victor Frankenstein in the role of the Ancient Titan, Prometheus, Mary Shelley's intentions were framed by the error of humanity taking on God's role that is alive in both the Promethean tale and the Genesis Creation narrative.

In the context of the Modern Prometheus, the creature's creator is seeking the creative spark as a mere mortal, thus playing with fire, and eating the fruit of the Tree. In his case, his behavior carried consequences as grave as those lived out by both Prometheus and Adam, for obvious reasons.

Dr. Frankenstein was to lament his creation of the monster, pushing it out into the world, where the homunculus sought a mate, laying waste to the land as it went. In the end, science went too far, stepping over the line between the material facility and the Creator's work.

In the literary incarnations, they're both most famous for, the Golem and Frankenstein are adjacent in time, with the Golem being about 50 years older than the Modern Prometheus. This proximity in time created the catalyst for mysticism to rear up in what was to become science fiction, born in the Romantic movement of which Shelley was part (with her husband, Percy Bysshe Shelley).

Creating a Monster

So, why have we ventured into talk of creating monsters as we discuss the Sefer Yetzirah? Simply. Simply, it's from this book that the Golem and other life forms are said to have been created, employing the linguistic mysticism and gematria (which we'll get into shortly) featured therein.

But to get to the bottom of how the Golem arose from the linguistic/numeric formula extant in its pages, we need to return to the Bible.

Specifically, we need to talk about a word in Psalm 139, which occurs nowhere else in the Hebrew Scriptures, in verse 16a – "galmi." The verse reads, "Your eyes beheld my unformed substance." While translated in the NRSV as "unformed substance," the Hebrew word "galmi" is translated from Babylonian Aramaic as an "incomplete vessel" or a "formless mass." A word in Syriac "galma" translates as "uncultivated soil."

Harkening back to the Creation of Adam from "Adamah" (the earth) in Genesis 2:7, humanity is depicted as the same unformed substance from which Creation was wrought in the Kabbalistic model. This was the "something" that "became" Creation due to the action of the Creator.

The root of the word "gimel, lamed, mem" is the same as that for "golem," and it's easy to see the connection between the "unformed substance" of the Psalmist and the mud doll of Genesis 2, into which the Creator breathed the Divine breath (ruach). The Talmud expands on the Creation narrative by timing the creation of humanity, saying, in Sanhedrin 38b, that the dust collected to create Adam became an "unformed substance" or galmi in the 4th hour of the Creation sequence. There is also a Midrashic treatment of Genesis 5:1b, specifically, "When God created humankind, he made them in the likeness of God." The Midrashic text describes Adam as a golem, ascribing tremendous size to him and depicting his figure as stretching from one end of the earth to the other.

So, in verse 16 of Psalm 139, what's being said by the Psalmist is that God saw the creatureliness of the writer as a golem – unformed substance that would not be a Son of God until it was animated by the Divine breath.

But it wasn't until the 13th Century that someone got it into his head to talk about the production of a golem, providing minutely detailed instructions following the Sefer Yetzirah. That was Rabbi Eleazar of Worms (1176 – 1238). Rabbi Eleazar is said to be the last of the Ashkenazi Hassidim of the original 13th Century flowering of the movement and a member of the original Kalonymos family, which arrived in the Rhineland from Italy.

Author of numerous Talmudic commentaries and mystical treatises in the Kabbalistic tradition, it was Eleazar of Worms who was to receive knowledge of the golem from Rabbi Yehuda ha Hassid (1150 – 1217), but it's also written that his father transmitted this knowledge to him. Eleazar of Worms was also the author of one of the most quoted commentaries on Sefer Yetzirah. But Rabbi Eleazar's Secrets of Mysticism of the Archangel Raziel (Sefer Razzael ha Malakh), also known as the Book of Solomon (in Latin), introduced the concept of creating life from the "32 paths of wisdom" in Sefer Yetzirah and the contents of the book's second chapter.

Raziel is an Archangel particular to the Kabbalah and known as the keeper of secrets and mysteries. In the sefirot, Raziel is associated with Chockmah and with the world of Beriah. The story of how the book of the Angel came to follow a familiar Kabbalistic trajectory, its contents being revealed to Adam and Eve at Creation.

Raziel is the Archangel who attends the Chariot/Throne, hearing all that's said and writing it down. The book's traditional tale sees it given to the Primordial Man and Woman after they've broken faith with God by eating from the Tree of the Knowledge of Good and Evil.

But not all Raziel's angelic colleagues were happy to hear of this attempt at education, so they took the book back, throwing it into the ocean. God, on hearing of all these angelic antics, resolved not to exact retribution on Raziel and sent the angel Rahab into the ocean to retrieve the book. God then returned the book to the Primordial Couple. The story is apocryphal, and it's easy to see clear parallels to Prometheus's story and his gift of fire to humans.

The story of transmission then shifts to Enoch, who appears in Genesis 5: 21 – 24, which concludes, "Enoch walked with God when he was no more because God took him." This is an allusion to ascension into the heavenly realm. So, the apocryphal tale has Enoch charging the Archangel Raphael with giving it to Noah (who used the wisdom to construct the Ark). And then, later, the book is said to have been given to Solomon (perhaps why the Latin text is called the Book of Solomon).

The Text

While the Book of the Angel Raziel is accredited to Eleazar of Worms, it's a collection of writings from a variety of authors. Most likely compiled by one author, the weaknesses of multiple authorship are revealed in contradictions in the text, occasioned by repeated transmission.

The book has three sections:

- Ha Malbush (the Book of the Garment, which refers to "putting on" the names of God
- The Great Raziel
- The Book of Secrets (Book of Noah)

Following these three sections, there are two brief sections, one entitled "creation" and one entitled "Shi'ur Komah" (Dimensions of the Body, in which God's body is "measured"), followed by formulas for incantations and amulets. Composition of the text is dated (at the earliest) to the 11th Century via language and type of content. The book itself was not printed until 1701, in Amsterdam.

Your Own Personal Golem

Making your own personal golem is no laughing matter, especially if you're using Rabbi Eleazar's complex formula.

I've entitled this chapter "Don't Try This at Home" because, well, you shouldn't! But if you're truly "touched" and have a burning passion for adding a golem to your household, it's going to require the support of a team, a lot of patience, and a good memory.

Because to pull this off, you'll be memorizing many formulas. You'll also need to speak thousands upon thousands of Hebrew phrases in the proper order and without flubbing your lines!

But before any of that happens, you must prep:

- Obtain soil from the earth that has never been dug
- Obtain spring water that has never been poured into any container
- Then, you'll need to mix the soil and water (because that's what your new friend is made of).

You and your golem-making team will also need to purify yourselves at the local mikveh (ritual bath) and don sparkling, clean, white clothing.

Then, there's the intentional breathing and head movements you'll all be making while combining all 22 letters of the Hebrew aleph-bet with each of the 4 letters of the Tetragrammaton (YHVH).

But before you do anything, you must choose between Rabbi Eleazar's instructions and those of Abraham Abulafia (1240 to sometime after 1291), which are far more complicated.

Put aside 7 to 35 hours to make yours!

The Golem of Prague

Undoubtedly the most celebrated of all the golemim, the Golem of Prague is a highly developed story about the consequences of making your own, personal golem.

Rabbi Judah Loew ben Bezalel (Between 1512 and 1526 - 1609) is credited with the production of this golem. Called the Maharal of Prague, Rabbi Loew's greatest claim to fame is undoubtedly the Golem of Prague, but he was also a highly respected Talmudic scholar, philosopher, and mystic.

The Golem of Prague's truth is that he wasn't really a "thing" until the 19th Century when the legend about Rabbi Loew began to be circulated. According to the legend, Rabbi Loew made his from the soil on the banks of the Vltava River. The accounts of the Prague Golem are recounted by several German writers from 1837 to 1847, with two earlier versions noted in 1834 and 1836

With all that in mind, let's read the story of the Golem of Prague, with an eye to understanding what golem-making is all about, and identifying the historical setting to understand why the tale was written.

The Story Goes...

The city of Prague in modern-day Czechoslovakia is an ideal setting for a tale like this; with its gothic spires and air of mystery, the golem could not possibly have emerged in the popular imagination in a more evocative place.

But the Prague of Rabbi Loew's times rejected the longstanding presence of the Jewish community (in existence there since at least the 10th Century). Many whispered about "magic" and attacks on Christian children. It was also rumored that the Jews of Prague found their way into the city's churches at night so they might destroy the consecrated host in the Tabernacle – the Body of Christ.

Because of the atmosphere of anti-Semitism, the Jews of Prague lived in difficult times. Poor, they had little power to repel the attacks which frequently befell them. Some Czechs even refused to sell basic necessities to the Jews – like food.

Rabbi Loew was a leader in the Jewish community, and he was greatly saddened to see what the people he led were forced to endure. Already expelled from Provence to Naples and then, from Laibach, Rabbi Loew felt that soon, Jews would also be expelled from Prague by the anti-Semitic Holy Roman Emperor, Rudolf II (1552 - 1612).

It happened one day that Rabbi Loew was sitting on the banks of the Vltava River. He was a busy and important man who spent most of his life helping other people, writing, and praying. But it was difficult for him to keep up with his duties, as he had no one to assist him in his work. He was feared because of his extreme holiness and intelligence. People didn't understand the Rabbi's fascination with biology and chemistry, believing these scientific disciplines to be dangerous and "ungodly." Many believed that Rabbi Loew was a magician.

Sitting on the riverbank, Rabbi Loew looked out at the spires of Prague. He wanted to protect the Jews of Prague but knew he had no hope of doing it alone.

As he gazed out over the city, the Rabbi saw a child playing on in the soil of the river, building a castle from the rich clay there. He had an idea.

"These people want to believe I'm a magician," he thought, "so, I will make them some magic!" It was at this very moment that Rabbi Loew resolved to create an assistant - one ready to support the Rabbi in all he did, whether in battle against the anti-Semites of Prague or in prayer.

The Rabbi collected a large quantity of the clay from the river's bank and took it to his home. Rabbi Loew toiled for weeks until he had formed a representation of a human form from the clay he had brought with him. He had constructed a type of clockwork on the interior of the figure but found that, despite his best efforts, his creation was still immobile and devoid of life.

The Rabbi thought of his studies and, after some reflection, inscribed the Holy Names of God on a scrap of paper. This was a mysterious name - impossible to pronounce. He rolled the paper into a scroll and placed it in the inanimate figure's mouth.

As he'd suspected, this action animated the creature, and it stumbled around the room, almost walking out an open window. The Rabbi laid hands on the creature, pulling the scroll from its mouth but still, it stumbled and lurched.

The Rabbi acknowledged there were bugs to work out with his prototype - but he was pleased with the result. "Finally!" he said, "I have created an assistant!"

But Rabbi Loew knew he had to treat his creature with extreme care. He called his creation "Golem" (unformed). He knew it wasn't human in God's eyes.

Initially, the Golem was tremendously helpful to the Rabbi. It helped around the house and could carry heavy loads and move large objects around. And now, when the anti-Semites came through the Prague Ghetto (where the Jews lived) to harass the people who lived there, it would come lurching out into the street and scare them away.

Over time, Rabbi Loew understood that he could communicate with the Golem telepathically to control it. He also figured out that if he didn't remember to remove the scroll from its mouth each night before going to bed that it would do what it wanted to.

Soon after this, Rabbi Loew was teaching at the synagogue. It was a cold day, and the children of the Ghetto were outside, playing. Passing by the Rabbi's house, they spied it through a window. Curious, they clicked their fingernails against the glass.

The Golem turned to look at them, which sent many running off in fear. But one child, unafraid, addressed it, saying, "Golem! We're cold! We'd like you to make us a fire!"

With this, the Golem got to work, launching itself out the window and smashing it in the process. The Rabbi had engineered his creation to do what was asked of it, and there was no innate will in the creature to prevent it from doing so. The moment its feet hit the ground, it collected tinder and built a fire. Soon, the fire had waxed large and warm, and the children, happy to no longer be cold, danced happily around it.

They called the Golem, saying, "Come dance with us!"

So, it danced with the children around the fire, as they laughed at this strange playmate and sang. As they danced, one child's voice rang out, "Golem, please make the fire bigger!"

Having tossed all the kindling it could find into the raging fire, it took some chairs from Rabbi Loew's house, breaking them into pieces and throwing them in. The fire was now enormous, and the children, afraid they'd gone too far, ran away.

In fact, the raging brazier built by the Golem caught one of the nearby buildings on fire and then another and another. But it didn't move a muscle. No one had asked it to put out the fire!

Finally, as the Golem watched, mute and slack-jawed, the fire was extinguished. In the aftermath, several houses were seen to have been burned to the ground. And the Golem was no more, consumed by the fire, with only the scorched scroll remaining as a testament to its existence. Prague's leading citizens were outraged, and the Emperor called for Rabbi Loew to appear before him and answer for the disaster.

The Rabbi was terrified. Bowing his head in prayer, he asked God to protect his people, even though he'd endangered them by allowing it to run amok. The Rabbi prayed and prayed for mercy, believing they would be put to death and that the Jews of Prague would be expelled from the city.

And so, Rabbi Loew went into the Emperor's presence with much fear and trembling. But when he saw Emperor Rudolf, he was beaming. He said to the Rabbi, "I understand that Jews are not permitted to create life, so please explain yourself to me."

Rabbi Loew, hesitant, decided at that moment to tell the Emperor the truth, saying, "That creature was not living. It was a doll; a facsimile of a human form which moved only by virtue of the Holy Name inserted in its mouth."

Emperor Rudolf was deeply intrigued, saying, "You know, Rabbi Loew, you're quite an interesting fellow and far too learned for me to kill. I will keep you captive, and while I do, you will create another creature like the other, only this time, for me."

Rabbi Loew's eyes grew large as the Emperor spoke. He knew this might be one of the many traps set by people like the Emperor.

Continuing, the Emperor said, "You will make me another creature. Because I have not seen the first Golem but have only heard of it, I'm having a difficult time believing it's real. If you're telling me the truth and the Golem does what it's supposed to, I'll set you free."

Rabbi Loew exhaled with relief.

But then, the Emperor said, "But if the Golem runs amok again, I will execute you, and the Jews of Prague will be expelled."

And so, Rabbi Loew bowed to the Emperor and ingratiated himself to him for his kindness. He was put into a comfortable but simple cell, and immediately, he began to work. The Golem he created was twice the size of the original model and massive in proportion, with huge, muscular arms and eyes that glowed red, like hot coals. When the Golem had been completed, Rabbi Loew brought it to the Emperor.

Standing before Emperor Rudolf, the Rabbi said, "This creature is made of simple clay and is driven by an internal mechanical system." Taking the animating scroll on which the Holy Name of God was inscribed, the Rabbi placed it in the creature's mouth, saying, "Watch this!"

Once the scroll was in the mouth of the Golem, it bowed to the Emperor.

Emperor Rudolf was ecstatic with his new acquisition, saying to the Rabbi, "I'm going to get a lot of use out of this Golem!"

But Rabbi Loew didn't feel right about the transaction. He said solemnly, "I'm sorry, Emperor, but I can't give you the Golem. It contains the Holy Name, and you're not a Jew. This might prove to be dangerous, as the creature may not do as you say and has the potential for enormous destruction."

The Emperor's face fell. He wasn't happy about losing his new toy before he'd even had a chance to use it. But his expression changed to his customary, beaming smile. The Rabbi wondered what was in this evil man's head.

"Evil men who smile so warmly should never be trusted," he thought silently. And in fact, the Emperor had a request for the Rabbi.

"Alright, Rabbi," said the Emperor. "I know I'm not a believer, but may I have a moment alone with the Golem?"

The Rabbi wasn't sure this was a good idea. He sensed that the Emperor would remove the scroll from its mouth. But the Rabbi also knew that if he refused the Emperor a private moment with the creature, that he might be killed. And so, Rabbi Loew said, "Of course, you can!"

The Emperor walked into another room with the Golem, returning after a few minutes. Then, he let Rabbi Loew leave, with it.

The Rabbi and the Golem returned to the Ghetto. The Rabbi was greeted with enthusiasm, as nobody had expected him to survive his visit to the Emperor. But it made them uneasy. Many stood far away, fearfully looking on. Observing this, Rabbi Loew realized he was increasingly seen as a magician. This worried him.

The Rabbi resolved to exercise caution with Golem 2.0. Before sundown, every Friday, he took the scroll bearing the Holy Name out of the mouth of it, ensuring that, like the Jews, it would rest.

As the days passed, the Golem became stronger, and its intelligence seemed to grow. The Rabbi was deeply impressed, as he hadn't anticipated this. With time, the Rabbi's community embraced the abilities of the Golem, and Rabbi Loew would even allow others to borrow it, with the proviso they get it back to him before sunset.

But then, something strange happened - something truly amazing. The Golem spoke!

It said, "I would like to be a soldier."

The Rabbi raised an eyebrow. "Why," he asked the Golem. "You could be anything you choose, so why a soldier?"

"Because I want to fight for my master," the Golem replied.

This confused Rabbi Loew. He said to the Golem, "I'm your master, and I don't want you to fight for me."

The Golem slowly shook its head from side to side, then said, "Not you. You are not my master. I will fight for my master, the Emperor."

The Rabbi was horrified by the Golem's words. Shaking with fear, he shouted, "Be silent!" The Golem closed his mouth and spoke no more.

The Rabbi then removed the scroll from the Golem's mouth and pondered what had effected this change. He knew that the Emperor had interfered with the Golem, and now, here it was, ready to go into battle.

The problem was, the Rabbi was on the verge of a breakthrough in the series of experiments he'd been conducting. He needed the Golem to run the equipment - the whole reason Rabbi Loew had made the thing in the first place!

So, with trepidation, the Rabbi continued using it as an assistant, as the Rabbi surveilled its behavior. It didn't speak anymore and became clumsy and dull-witted. The Rabbi noted that it responded to commands listlessly. And Rabbi Loew searched his soul. "Have I sinned in creating this thing?" he asked himself.

But here the Golem was, and Rabbi Loew didn't know what he would do with it, after all this time. "How would I manage without it?" he wondered.

As time passed, it behaved normally. Once again, it was obeying the Rabbi's commands, and never again did it speak. The Rabbi was relieved, believing that the rebellion of the Golem had passed.

But there was one strange thing about its behavior. Every night, it would heave huge lumps of clay from the riverbank, piling them up outside the Rabbi's house. Rabbi Loew couldn't make heads or tails of it, but the lumps of clay didn't interfere with anything, so he let it go. But in the back of his mind was a fearful thought - was the Golem gathering an army of creatures like himself?

Then, one Friday afternoon, as the Rabbi was getting ready to leave for the synagogue, there was a resounding crash outside. And he heard a voice calling, "Rabbi, hurry! Your monster is trying to break into the synagogue!"

Rabbi Loew hurried out into the street and, arriving at the doors of the synagogue, yelled, "Stop, Golem!"

But the Golem continued pounding its massive fists against the synagogue door. The Rabbi was beside himself as he shouted, "What is this? What are you trying to prove?"

The Golem turned to the Rabbi, red eyes blazing in his enormous head, saying, "The Holy Law must be destroyed! I will get into the synagogue and destroy it, and then, I will be beyond your control. I will make other golemim to fight for our master, and we will become an army to destroy the Jews of Prague!"

It was then that the Rabbi knew, with certainty, of his sin. He also knew that he'd been correct about those lumps of clay the Golem had been collecting. Outraged and penitent, he pointed at it, shouting, "Monster!"

Throwing himself at the raging Golem, the Rabbi reached up, trying to get the scroll from its mouth, but with its huge hand, the creature pushed the Rabbi away, and he was thrown to the ground.

But the people of the Ghetto had gathered around in the commotion and began to attack the Golem, as it struggled against them. A child in the crowd climbed up on its back. Once it had reached the creature's shoulders, it reached into its mouth and pulled out the scroll.

The effect on the Golem was immediate. As the child scrambled to the ground, it crumbled into pieces. As the crowd cheered, Rabbi Loew got on his knees to beg their forgiveness.

"Oh, my people, how I have transgressed against you! In my arrogance, I erred and risked all our lives!" The Rabbi hung his head in shame with the weight of his sin.

But the people were forgiving. They knew the Rabbi had been trying to help and said, "You created the Golem with the best intentions, Rabbi! But we have learned an important lesson – that we can't depend on a Golem to protect us from those who hate us. That's up to us!"

The crumbled pieces of the Golem were gathered and placed in the synagogue's attic, where it could do no more harm and where it might be remembered for the lesson it had brought the Jews of Prague.

And ever after, Rabbi Loew was remembered for the tale of the Golem.

The Moral of the Story

You already know the moral of the story, as we started this chapter by recounting Prometheus's stories (punished by having his eternally regenerating liver eaten daily by an eagle) and of Frankenstein (punished by the very force he unleashed when he created a monster).

Good intentions gone horribly awry similarly mark Rabbi Loew's tale. In his zeal to find the scientific answer to protecting his people, he found an agent of chaos instead.

The story's moral is simple enough – don't play with fire, and you won't get burned. In the instance of Prometheus and the origin of the expression "don't play with fire", fire was making a benevolent gift of something the gods wanted exclusively for themselves. Why? Because they didn't believe humans could be trusted with it. In Dr. Frankenstein's case, fire was the creation of a living being he had no true understanding of. He could not have known that his monster would develop an emotional life and that his emotions would run amok. In the same way, Rabbi Loew created a monster, intended to help him in his work and, ultimately, in saving his people. He could not have known that the Emperor would turn his creation on him and the Jews of Prague.

And that is the whole point. As we read in Sirach 3:23 (in the Deuterocanonical or Apocryphal books): "Do not meddle in matters that are beyond you, for more than you can understand has been shown you."

Don't play with fire. You might get burned.

In the pages of the Sefer Yetzirah and Sefer ha Bahir, you'll find the makings of the golem, in all its incarnations. But what are these makings rooted in? What is the secret sauce that results in the clay homunculus?

In our next chapter, we'll talk about linguistic mysticism and gematria and how they characterize these early works of Kabbalah, influencing the entire canon.

Chapter Seven: The Mysticism of Letters and Numbers

"I love mysticism! It's such fun!" **Jerry Hall**

Fun! Mysticism certainly is fun, especially when you tend to wear your beard longer than the average mystic. It can be said that mysticism is a source of great joy for those with the diligence and patience to approach it with the respect it deserves.

I have nothing against the lovely Jerry Hall. As a matter of fact, I rather admire her willingness to admit to giving mysticism the time of day. But then, I remember that mysticism is readily reduced to the level of the flavor of the month by people who run in Jerry's circles, if only concentrically.

Mysticism has seen a cycle in recent years of being a celebrity hobby. Red string and holy water happy, the Kabbalah Center boasted a following of luminaries as notable as Madonna and Alex Rodriguez. Celebrities fairly flocked to it.

But the version of mysticism marketed by the Kabbalah Center is like the prosperity gospel – promises of unlimited happiness and success are made, if only you will believe. An illustrative instance of my intention here is the belief that merely scanning the texts of

Kabbalah is considered sufficient in this movement for one to be spiritually transformed. And that is without understanding them or even reading them in their original Hebrew or Babylonian Aramaic

Individual spiritual transformation leading to personal prosperity is the opposite of mysticism's basis, which is universal healing and the aim of ultimate union with the Divine for the whole Created Order. This is common to mystical thinking in all religions.

So, before we discuss the mysticism of letters and numbers, we need to take a little detour to remember what we're talking about – the Sefer Yetzirah. The fact that this book is one of the Jewish World's most-read religious texts of all time is incredible. Not just due to its age but due to its cryptic language and intensely esoteric nature, the greatest of sages has found in Sefer Yetzirah reason to write commentaries in the thousands, confronting its mysteries.

A mystical text rooted in the revolution and cataclysm of Creation, the Sefer Yetzirah is what mysticism is all about – the complex relationship of things, why they are this way, and how we figure in the plan of perfecting them. Mysticism's co-creative battle plan is routinely to re-unite humanity with its Divine source and to think it into being through poetry, song, verse, scripture, and maybe even the backs of cereal boxes. Mysticism goes that deep and that detailed. Because with mysticism, all those details add up to God.

And mystics, as part of their service to and joy in the Creator, are compelled in spirit to spread the love, to get closer to the heart of the truth they're seeking and to the cure for the common shevirah.

Anyone who believes mysticism to be wishful or magical thinking, perpetuated by mad wizards and wanton faeries, should probably keep reading. The intellectual power behind the Sefer Yetzer and our understanding of it, through numerous commentaries, is humbling and a testament to the diligent pursuit after humanity by the Hounds of whatever heaven you believe in.

Let me share with you the fact that linguistic mysticism in the canon of Kabbalah is how Natural Language Processing (NLP) in Artificial Intelligence was born. Here's the story.

Most believe that Alan Turing (1912 – 1954) discovered NLP in 1950, framing it as the ability of a machine to coherently interface with a human. This belief rests on NLP being purely a data-driven reality. But our understanding is missing a piece.

Abraham Abulafia (1240 – Circa 1291)

In the late 13th Century, Abraham Abulafia combined the letters of the aleph-bet in nonsensical and seemingly inconsequential ways. This was not a compulsion. It was a spark of inspiration.

This was to become his life's work – interpreting the prescriptions of the Sefer Yetzirah and the voluminous collection of commentaries about it. The system of letters he produced was the basis for his Science of Language.

By interpreting the prescriptions found in Sefer Yetzirah, Abulafia had developed his own rulebook from what was written there, especially regarding the formation of Creation through the agency of the Hebrew aleph-bet.

What Abraham Abulafia discovered is that the rearrangement of letters often renders unseen meaning. Through this discovery, he produced a series of writings that were proverbs he'd rendered, using this system. These, he claimed, were endowed with prophecy. He'd spent months upon months combining letters in select texts and coming forth with new interpretations that lay just below the surface of the text – the inner soul.

Abulafia's premise was that the aleph-bet's mystical treatment revealed truths that were not touched on by the visible, written word, but that these were only the beginning of what was possible. Beneath the words, he insisted, was a much deeper meaning.

Indeed, the Sefer Yetzirah was a somewhat feared book in some religious circles. At the center of that disagreement was our friend from the last chapter – the golem. Rabbi Loew's golem was created via the formula interpreted by Abraham Abulafia in the 13th Century, following the Sefer Yetzirah. Tales arose – cautionary tales – about the golem. Some were innocent enough, with Rabbis said to have made golemim of livestock (chickens, cows) for food. In others, it turns on the Rabbi. As we saw in the Tale of the Golem of Prague, it turned on the Jews due to the interference of the Emperor.

And this is perhaps why the Golem of Prague is the most famed of the golemim. Having turned on the Jews, the moral of the story becomes clear – creation is in the hands of the Divine and messing with that imperative is a dangerous game.

Dangerous, especially when you're talking about the stuff of Creation – the aleph-bet.

But today, Sefer Yetzirah is almost universally revered and studied intensely by people of many faith systems. And its role in the history of Artificial Intelligence, via NLP, indisputable, with Abulafia's Science of Language standing in witness.

While Abraham Abulafia clarified that combining Hebrew letters rendered knowledge and a deeper understanding of the texts they were pulled from, he also knew their power. That power is expressed in the many cautionary tales of the golem and the danger inherent, in the mystical mind, in messing with the letters of the aleph-bet.

They're the stuff of Creation, as you'll remember, and so the double-edged sword of Abulafia's explorations is even apparent today.

It was in the human intellect that Natural Language Processing was born, challenging post-modernist appeals to the superiority of machine over human. Regardless, it may yet be in the digital world we find the 21st Century's version of the Tower of Babel – that double-edged sword.

As you've seen, there's nothing simple-minded about mysticism – especially the mysticism of and around the Sefer Yetzirah. This book's interpretation has rendered numerous commentaries, books, films, newspaper articles, television shows, and websites.

That's not bad for an ancient, esoteric book.

Now, let's get into a discussion about the linguistic mysticism of the Sefer Yetzirah and the Word as Creation.

Spoken into Being

The power of language is part of the fabric of the Creation narrative in the Book of Genesis. Reverence for the *Word* of God is about what's *written down*, but it's much more keenly invested in the power of that Word. In this instance, the power to create. But the Word, in the Biblical Creation Narrative, goes much deeper than that.

The Word is part of everything Creation is - a veil over the potency of its concealed, patiently waiting source, with the Word representing the material presence of God, as God watches from a safe distance.

A convenient window into the philosophy of language's power is found in the philosophy underlying the formulation of the Tetragrammaton (YHVH). This was arrived at as a fitting means by which God might be identified in the text. The reasoning follows expressions of linguistic power in the Creation narrative – that what can be named is limited. A good demonstration of that point is in the naming of the sun and moon by God, in the Creation narrative (Genesis 1:16), calling them "greater light to rule the day and the lesser light to rule the night – and the stars."

The intention is to diminish the Pagan role of the sun and moon as objects of worship. By giving them deliberately reductionist names and clearly delineating their "turf," the sun and moon are put in their places under the One God rule. Cast as lighting fixtures, the divine power is not only stripped of them but roundly mocked. By being named, they become limited.

The Tetragrammaton provides a cover for the Holy Names of God, expressed as just three letters – yud, hey, and vav, with hey repeated twice - YHVH. Like the Ark of the Covenant, it bears within it the Limitless Truth, which can't be fully named, fully understood, or fully confronted.

So, through the deployment of language, the hidden God instigates Creation. This is the ultimate demonstration of both linguistic power and linguistic mysticism, with language centered as an active agent of God in Creation.

In Sefer Yetzirah, it's specifically in the 22 numbers of the aleph-bet and the 10 cardinal numbers that Creation is accomplished. Its formulas, whether making a golem or revealing the secrets of the Torah, take on a life of their own and a deeply mystical nature which has riveted Jewish mystics for centuries.

More on Naming

Sefer Yetzirah and Sefer ha Bahir feature numerous lists of Angel names and the names of God. In the 13th Century Spain of Abraham Abulafia, these were studied intensely and were accompanied by numeric equations.

The practice of assigning a numeric value to letters provided another interpretative layer. Some mystics believed that studying these formulae would lead them to the ability to influence the life of the Divine realms. But Abulafia, with his Science of Language, believed he'd found an interpretive method, based on intellectual exploration, to gain access to the most profound depths of the texts of not just Sefer Yetzirah but of the entire canon of Jewish religious literature. He further believed that his system of linguistic mysticism was how the practitioner could obtain spiritual unification with God.

In those names, Abulafia believed, was the healing of Creation so long-awaited - tikkun olam. By apprehending the truth of language's mystical power, the mystic was uniquely positioned to speed up the process of bringing about the intended state of what the Divine had built.

A Temple of the Spirit

Moshe Idel is an Israeli historian and philosopher of Jewish Mysticism. His theory about the reification (materialization) of language in Jewish Mysticism harkens back to the destruction of the First and then the Second Temple. He believes that the position of language in this context was the foundation of a new and inviolable Temple.

The position of language in Judaism and the intense reverence for the Word as a means of seeking God is clear, but when that language is reified, it becomes something more powerful - connected to the source of the First Speaker (God). In each word and letter is the cornerstone of Judaism, building a Temple of the spirit. Stone by stone, this indestructible Temple is built. But those stones are words and the letters which compose them.

In Idel's theory, the ritual sacrifices practiced in the Ancient Temples are replaced by prayers lifted by the faithful. With spirituality as its context, the deployment of language is the answer to the shevirat ha-kelim - tikkun. In imitation of God's creative actions, the praying community of devotion calls on the power of language to repair what has been damaged through its prayerful disciplines.

Words become stones in this model, reassembling the Temple in the hearts of the people and, in so doing, perfecting Creation. In its materialization, language becomes a Divine tool in the hands of the Jewish mystics, with prayer as the raw material - the words building a Creation healed of its primordial wound.

The belief in the material power of language is central to 18th Century Hassidism (building on the work of Abulafia, among many others). But its roots are deeply embedded in the Jewish faith. But it's in Hasidism that the true, material power of language is seen as a spiritual bridge between God and humanity and the reclaiming of the ancient Temple becomes a spiritual reality, living in the hearts of believers.

Language as a Creative Agent

In Sefer Yetzirah, the Hebrew aleph-bet is framed as even more than a collective emissary of the Divine. These letters form the Created Order. There is no separating the aleph-bet from the Creation or the Creation from the aleph-bet.

Sefer Yetzirah further casts the Hebrew language as that of God, thus bearing as cosmic significance over and above that of any other language. Woven into the stuff of Creation, Hebrew, in Sefer Yetzirah, stands as a creative agent, issuing directly from the mouth of the Creator.

Formed in the second sefirah (Chokhmah/Wisdom), the aleph-bet is manipulated by God in the narrative, in the same way, it was to be manipulated by Abraham Abulafia in the 13th Century. Combining all 22 letters of the aleph-bet as a creative method is depicted in Sefer Yetzirah as the creation's work.

And while Abulafia later claimed the same methodology, what he was creating was a series of books derived from other writings. The Divine was creating the universe, which is a unique prerogative (as we've seen with the Golem of Prague).

Language in Heikhalot

The Heikhalot texts of the early Merkavah Mysticism tradition are another key locus for apprehending the importance of language in Kabbalah. In these texts, God's name is intrinsic to God, being of one substance with the Divine. The Tetragrammaton is described as "consubstantial" – indivisible from its source and integrated into the Divine's total meaning and vice versa. The most Holy Name is Holy because *it is the Holy itself*.

Heikhalot goes further than this, though, characterizing every letter of the aleph-bet as a name of God. This concept is seen throughout Kabbalistic traditions, but most vibrantly in Sefer Yetzirah, with the aleph-bet acting not just as agents of Creation but as its very substance. This represents the reification of language in the earliest layer of Kabbalah, in the investment of Divine agency. But in this reification is also a physical and spiritual link, uniting human prayers with Divine nature. In the ground we walk on, in the air we breathe, in the water we drink, bathe in, and water our crops with, there is the language of God, and there is God's living presence in Creation.

Not only bearing God's energy but acting as influences on the Created Order, the aleph-bet, having issued from the Divine, in inspiration, Word, and action stands as the concealed God's very presence among us.

Visual Kabbalah

Hebrew characters in their graphic form stand as symbols of the sefirot (emanations of the Divine), and names of God. Because of this role, any changes to the shape of the letters would be viewed as a heretical act, distorting the image of God.

Whether written or spoken, the reified Hebrew aleph-bet of Jewish Mysticism transcends what is said in the text or arrived at in subsequent interpretations. A great significance is attached to the forms of the letters and the white space on which they're written. The distance between the symbol and the symbolized is eliminated, and the Hebrew characters are Holy icons. This is key to understanding the mystical experience of language and its sacred power, according to Kabbalah.

Nehunya ben HaKanah, the same First Century author the Sefer ha Bahir was attributed to by Nachmanides, is the most likely author of the Sefer ha-Temunah (Book of the Image, most commonly dated to the 13th Century). This book is an exploration of the mystical nature of Hebrew characters, interpreting and presenting them as sefirotic symbols. Presumed to have been produced by the same author, Sod Shem ha-Meforash (The Secret of the Tetragrammaton) is another book that outlines the basis for linguistic mysticism in Kabbalah. Tantalizingly, whoever wrote the Sefer ha Temunah asserted that one letter was missing from the Hebrew aleph-bet and this would only be revealed after Creation was healed.

This letter connects, according to interpretative commentaries, to Creation's flaws. Some interpretations credit the revelation of this "missing" letter with the satisfaction of tikkun, as it will change the nature of language, making new words possible and ushering in the state of perfection Creation was intended to model.

Some say that the letter shin is the missing letter but only in the version of the character which appears on the box containing the tefillin. Only for this application does this letter appear with 4 prongs and not 3. In this scenario, the pronunciation of this version of shin, with the revelation of the Divine Name, will initiate the final stages of tikkun.

Closely associated with linguistic mysticism is gematria, a system of assigning numeric values to letters, which supports the deeper understanding of Jewish religious texts.

A Numbers Game

When you're talking about gematria, you're talking about a Greek precedent, also called "isopsephy." In theoretical practice, values are assigned to individual letters to arrive at a numeric value for the word they form. Employing gematria as an additional layer of interpretation, the resulting numbers point to a spiritual significance in the text, which is otherwise unstated.

The practice itself goes back to Tannaitic times, according to sources in Mishnah (Pirkei Avot 3: 23) and in the Talmud (Sanhedrin 22a).

The Mispar is the guide by which gematria is applied, existing in 2 versions – the hechrechi (absolute value) and the Mispar gadol (larger value). According to the prescriptions in the Misparim, Hebrew characters have a value of 1 to 9, at the beginning of the aleph-bet (aleph through tet) and then from 10 through 90 (yud through tzady). Following that, characters are assigned values from 100 to 400 (kuf through taf). Finally, the "sofit" characters (forms of letters which end words, i.e., "mem sofit") are assigned values in multiples of 100, from 500 through 900 (kaf sofit through tzady sofit), but this only applies to Mispar gadol. Mispar hechrechi assigns no value to the word-ending version of Hebrew characters.

Vowels are not assigned values in these two principles gematria guides. Expressed as "pointings" (which indicate the vowel taken by the collection of consonants in play), they're rarely assigned a numeric value, although there are many versions of the two foundational Misparim which *do* assign them a numeric value.

A good example of gematria and a simple one is the word "chai" (alive). Consisting of two letters (yud and het). According to the Mispar, yud has a value of 10 and het, a value of 8, adding up to 18. But the real fun starts when you add the 1 and the 8, arriving at the word's final value, which is "9". This number (18) may also be doubled to 36, called "double chai" (and 3 plus 6 equals 9).

The number 9 is also the sum of the gematria of the name of Primordial Man, "Adam."

Aleph has a value of 1, dalet, a value of 4, and mem sofit, a value of 40. These numbers added together equal 45. And what do 4 and 5 add up to?

Nine.

Attend a Jewish wedding and provide a gift of money to the happy couple. You'll get extra points for gifts that are multiples of 9 or which add up to 9 – like 1 and 8. Remember: there are 9 cardinal numbers, with 10 being the number of Creation.

Now, try to multiply any number by 9. The result will render a number that can be reduced to 9.

$$9 \times 9 = 81. \ 8 + 1 = 9$$

$$5 \times 9 = 54. \ 5 + 4 = 9$$

While you won't find many references to the number nine in the traditional canon of Jewish or Kabbalistic religious literature, there is a quality to the number which has adhered to social traditions, and 18 is considered by Jews to be the luckiest number of all. It's also notable that the Chanukiah (Hanukkah menorah) has nine branches.

Joseph ben Abraham Gikatilla (1248 – After 1305)

Closely related to exegesis (which is the study of scripture, applying parallel texts against the one being interpreted), hermeneutics is interpreted primarily from four distinct standpoints – literal, moral, and anagogical and allegorical.

While the hermeneutics' practice cannot be said to fall under the rubric of linguistic mysticism, it is an interpretative method that may be guided by it through the anagogical method (analogous to "sod" in Judaism). And in this method, Kabbalah has a 13th Century exemplar in Joseph Gikatilla, a student of Abraham Abulafia's.

Also known as "Baal ha Nissim" (Master of Miracles), some said that his mastery of Kabbalah rendered him able to performs miracles. Following the word of his teacher, Abulafia, Gikatilla was adept at producing the same letter combinations as his master, and being skilled at gematria.

But Gikatilla was most profoundly concerned with philosophy. As a sage, his primary objective was to reconcile the teachings of philosophy with those of Kabbalah. In truth, his work focused on developing philosophical insight into the mysticism of Kabbalah, as Gikatilla considered philosophy to be the basis for mysticism, placing mysticism (in his thinking) in the position of a "higher science."

Writing prolifically, his first work was entitled "Gannat E'goz" (meaning "Garden of Nuts"). But the intent of the title is far more interesting than nuts could ever be, even were one a squirrel.

The word "Ginnat" comprises the root gimmel-nun-tau, representative of the 3 interpretive pillars of Kabbalah – gematria, notarikon, and temurah. "E'goz" means "nut" in Hebrew, and the nut is the symbol of mysticism. Even in Christian Mysticism, Julian of Norwich (English Anchorite and mystic, 1343 – after 1416) wrote of the hazelnut in her Revelations of Divine Love, saying, "It is all that is made." Small and seemingly inconsequential, this creaturely expression contains the fullness of the Created Order.

And so, the Ginnat E'goz is an exploration of "all that is made" using the formulas of Kabbalah. We've reviewed gematria. Now, let's explore the methodologies of Notarikon and Temurah.

Notarikon

Deriving from Greek, the Greek word itself was previously derived from the Latin, "notarius," which means "writer of shorthand".

In this method of exploring the deeper meaning of religious texts, the first and final letters of a word are utilized to represent another, forming a sentence of an idea out of the words being manipulated. Another method repeats this process - or - substitutes the two letters in the middle of a word, forming another word.

This method was used extensively by Rashi (Schlomo Yitchaki, 1040 - 1105). Rashi lived, studied, and wrote in France's Medieval Era, authoring exemplary commentaries on the Talmud and Tanakh. A master of peshat, Rashi is the straight talker of sages, shedding light for both neophytes and the learned. For this reason, his body of work continues to play a central role in 21st Century Jewish study.

If you haven't guessed, the point I'm making here is that anything that's good enough for Rashi is good enough for the rest of us. Rashi's work rationalism makes this an interesting wrinkle and a welcome one in the discussion of Sefer Yetzirah and linguistic mysticism. Linguistic mysticism is not limited to the mystical side of the global Jewish community.

In Kabbalistic terms, notarikon is used to form God's sacred names from either Biblical or other sources in the greater canon.

Temurah

It is a similar, letter-based technique that seeks the same goal – Divine revelation in the Holy, Creation-infusing letters of the Hebrew aleph-bet.

There are three methods in temurah of doing so:

- **Atbash** – The first letter of a word is replaced with the last letter of the aleph-bet and the second letter of the word, replaced with the second to last letter, and so on until the word has been transformed to reveal its hidden meaning.

- **Avgad** – Each letter of any given the word is replaced with the letter before it.

- **Albam** – The first letter of the alphabet, where it occurs, is replaced with the 12th and the second with the thirteenth, etc.

Cikatilla mastered the three methodologies, thus establishing his command of Kabbalah, as witnessed by the book we're discussing, Ginnat Egoz. But his enormous body of work is crowned by the book, Sha'are Orah (Gates of Light).

In this work, Cikatilla's mysticism drives a text of intense passion and a stunning example of linguistic mysticism in its own right. Renowned for centuries, this book has been singled out by some of religious Judaism's most respected historical voices. Isaac Luria, for example, said it was a "key to understanding" mysticism. The Vilna Gaon recommended it to his students, and it's quoted extensively by luminaries like Moses Cordovero and Chaim Vital.

Sha're Orah is a complex exploration of God's names, utilizing the standard Kabbalistic methods, connecting those sacred names to the sefirot, sometimes to more than one.

And the spirit in which the book is offered says a lot about where the author was coming from "so that you can understand the 'Fountain of Living Waters' that flows from all (God's) names, and when you attain this, then you will prosper and have good success." From Gikatilla's introduction to the book, this snippet references Jeremiah 2: 13 and Joshua 1: 8.

There is almost an evangelistic zeal in Gikatilla's words, but a friendly one, which genuinely seeks the glory of tikkun and the perfection of this aleph-bet soup that is Creation.

Next, I'd like to talk a little about current discussions about the book, its role in popular culture, and how it serves to educate people about the Jewish Faith.

Chapter Eight: A Golem Points the Way

Had I not written this book; I might have lived my whole life not knowing that the Northern California Jewish News features a column by "Astrolojew." The best part of this column, from my standpoint, is this Jewish astrology columnist references Sefer Yetzirah in his weekly prognostications.

And the Astrolojew is not alone. Sefer Yetzirah has seen incredible interest in recent decades, from traditional (non-mystically oriented) Judaism and those outside the Tradition, including those from other religious Faith systems. Mysticism seems to have come of age, waking up in a strange and unknown land. Maybe it's the spiritual vacuity of post-modernistic creep (from Kurzweil to "intimate" companion dolls), but there is a hunger abroad in the land, and Sefer Yetzirah is enjoying something of a renaissance.

The wonder of the studious approach to sacred texts prevalent in universal Judaism, mystical or not, is that it multiplies the available body of knowledge. It's only for this reason that Sefer Yetzirah is so widely available and avidly pursued in the modern age. Centuries of wisdom have explored its depths, both by means of advanced hermeneutical techniques specific to Kabbalistic study and interpretation and by traditional hermeneutics. The canon derived from Sefer Yetzirah is vast, varied, and challenging to penetrate.

The centuries of revealed wisdom left by the sages have made the contents of the Sefer Yetzirah accessible to those who don't read the original Hebrew. Via their detailed and revelatory commentaries, the modern world has been provided with a window to understanding.

This is both blessing and curse, as it is whenever an ancient, spiritually based system or practice is popularized. Strange eruptions occur in locations far off the beaten path. These usually involve some syncretic (the interpolation of one religion's beliefs/practices into another) activity or even cult activity (when the lessons of a Faith are popularized for controlling an adoring flock).

But in the blessing column is that Sefer Yetzirah – and Jewish Mysticism, in general – have stood in almost ambassadorial roles on behalf of Judaism. By increasing understanding of proximity of beliefs in adjacent systems in the Ancient Near East, we come to a much closer understanding of relatedness and the common purpose of all our beliefs. This is a unique basis for ecumenism and mysticism.

But with its unique intellectual approach to spirituality, Kabbalah holds a special attraction in our increasingly strange and challenging age, appealing to the rationality and data-derived flight from humanity represented by post-modernity. But concurrently, Kabbalah inspires the romanticism of those who long for something deeper than zeros and ones.

The numbers are there, in gematria. NLP is in Abraham Abulafia's work. But on top of that lies the story of Creation and humanity's purpose in it. This reaches beyond the metallic shell of our time, bringing the seeker, whether romantic or intellectual, a version of metaphysics that honors both impulses while challenging the spirit to move forward.

And then, there are the proponents of Jewish energy healing and psychics.

A 2019 article in the Jewish Journal recounts a rather strange tale, told in great earnest by its author, Marcus J. Freed. In it, he speaks of discovering a variety of people in his community undergoing various psychic experiences and phenomena. He speaks of the fact that traditional Judaism isn't crazy about Jewish energy healers, psychics, and others in that vein. But then he says, "A frequent question I hear when teaching Jewish concepts is, "How can I become more psychic?" This is the wrong question. There are warnings around studying Jewish mysticism, and these warnings have merit."

He describes the descent into catatonia of a client who had hired someone to assist in "opening his third eye" by employing the study of Kabbalah. The client was admitted to the Psychiatric Ward twice.

A very strange tale, but really, it has nothing on the Golem when you think about it. Indeed, Kabbalah can be dangerous if misused, which is why you should not venture into the production of a Golem at home – or that of a "third eye" (just to be safe).

Everyone has their way to God; true. That's not our concern here. Our concern is rather with the Sefer Yetzirah and Kabbalah when it arrives in the public domain and its effect. Those effects can be myriad and more than a little weird in a world filled with spiritual hunger. While the examples above are interesting and (hopefully) fun to reflect on, the circulation of the book in popular culture and the impact that has is our purpose, so let's turn to that.

Sefer Yetzirah busts out in places you'd expect it to (Israel) and places you never would (Los Angeles). In Israel, vocalist Victoria Hanna released the single, Aleph-Bet in 2015. The song sings through the Aleph-Bet, becoming the prayer for rain from the Hashonot (meaning "Hosanna") service for Sukkot's liturgy. Another of Hanna's songs from the same year is entitled "22 Letters," and then there's "Sefer Yetzirah," so it's clear where this Israeli singer's heart is.

Principally known for giving voice to ancient mystical texts, Hanna said in a recent interview, "The mouth is a tool of Creation, and every letter is a specific tool." She continues this line of thought, saying,

"When you say all the letters in order, you create something in the world."

If you've read this far, Victoria Hanna's apparent mission in her sung spiritual art is to "create something in the world." This was in precisely the same way that ancient sages continuously study, interpret, and comment on the texts of Kabbalah, and have engaged in that mission for many centuries, ever praying into being the return of the Messiah and realization of tikkun olam.

In Los Angeles, the Kabbalah Center features the Sefer Yetzirah on its website, describing it as "Authored by Abraham the Patriarch. It is the oldest written document in our possession today that outlines a path to regain control over this physical world, and ultimately our destiny."

In this one brief quotation, it's not that difficult to ascertain the spiritual impetus of the Kabbalah Center. The traditional authorship of Oral Tradition is honored. But that's where the comparisons to Jewish Mystical thinking about Sefer Yetzirah end.

Claiming that the Sefer Yetzirah shows us how to "regain control over this physical world" may be a capsule way of saying "collaborate in the achievement of tikkun." So, we can give the Kabbalah Center the benefit of the doubt for a moment. But when the text continues by framing what is intended to be tikkun in the Kabbalistic sense (the healing of the relationship between God and humanity, resulting in perfection) as "our destiny," it rather removes all doubt. Individualism and a concurrent control fetishism are expressed, making the Kabbalah Center's appeal to popular neurosis obvious.

This ties in closely to the Kabbalah Center's emphasis on personal prosperity and wellness as rewards for studying Kabbalah (in a manner of speaking). For only $52.00 (the cost for an English language version of Sefer Yetzirah on the KC website), you too can control your environment – your ultimate destiny! Perhaps I'm being churlish, but the individualism in the product description is breathtaking, considering Kabbalah's communitarian focus.

From an article entitled Abraham the Patriarch and discussing Sefer Yetzirah, dated February 07, 2012 (also on the website): "There lies the secret behind the Book of Formation: Abraham's work contains all the spiritual equations concerning our world of time, space, and motion. The Book of Formation contains the secrets of existence, from the origins of life to the origins of the chaos that afflicts mankind."

Breathless and newsy, the Sefer Yetzirah is sold as a ticket to a cosmic amusement park, mirroring the language of commerce.

And this is the double-edged sword of spiritual populism. As the world has discovered that these books exist, it has hungrily identified opportunities for "development" which might be spiritual. But there are other problems associated with popularity.

Transhumanism getting in on the act, for example, via the Golem.

Missing the Point

A 2012 article in HPlus Magazine had this to say of the Golem: "The Golem, the Homunculus – most have never heard of these terms...The men behind these ideas, seeking immortality and superior human abilities and powers, were the ideological predecessors of the transhumanist movement."

Besides the fact that the transhumanists, an offshoot of post-modernism driven largely by the work of Ray Kurzweil, author of The Age of Spiritual Machines, in which humans become "disembodied" and immortal, have missed the point. They've mistaken the Sefer Yetzirah as the locus classicus of humanity's drive toward the lofty heights of the Tower of Babel.

The point being missed is that the presumed pretension to immortality (not a Jewish belief, by any means) and to human "superiority" in terms of abilities is not at all what Sefer Yetzirah had in mind. As we recall from the chapter on the Golem, there was a moral to the most famous of the Golem narratives, as there is to most. There is a distinct prohibition against the creation of life due to that function's assignment to God and God alone. The transhumanists are, in fact, pointed in the opposite direction to which the Golem points as the way.

The transhumanists eagerly await the demise of humans as we yield to the robots, hoping that the Sefer Yetzirah is a guidebook to the perfection of the original clay doll of Genesis, a sort of "Golem-Making 101".

While growing to prominence in the mid-20th Century, that humanity could be improved upon through digital and mechanical interventions has been around since at least 1921, when Czech playwright Karel Capek (1890 – 1938) wrote the play R.U.R. (Rossom's Universal Robots). He drew on the tale of the Golem. It was Capek's play which introduced the word "robot" to the world and into the canon of modern science fiction, a genre Capek was celebrated for.

Capek's idea was that robots would stand-in for humans as a labor force, taking on all the physically demanding tasks best performed by workers made of circuitry and data. You can see in Cupek's intention to create laborers; Rabbi Loew's to produce an assistant. Innocent enough, right? But the most innocent, even noble, plans can go horribly awry, as we've seen in the Prague Golem's story.

Capek later denied that he'd modeled R.U.R. on the Golem of Prague (where he lived), but the similarities in the plot and thematics make it clear he did. The play affirms the usefulness of robots as labor-saving devices but pauses to ask the philosophical question about what effect they might have on human life. So, while we wonder if Capek's work hasn't been perhaps misappropriated by transhumanism, it seems that his heart was in the right place.

Posthumanism and Transhumanism – The World of Golemim

Capek's intentions did not stop the emerging push to create artificial intelligence and to enshrine it as an evolutionary step for humanity. In the same way the Golem has been co-opted by transhumanism, so the word "robot" has been co-opted to transcend the human body and its limitations.

Transhumanism, or the idea that our human limitations may be transcended, using technological interventions, has been around as a theme for centuries (with Shelley's Modern Prometheus joining Varied Reflections on the Fountain of Youth - William Godwin et al.'s arguments for physical immortality). But not until 2002 did the Transhumanist Declaration come to be.

What is most striking about the Declaration is its acknowledgment that change can run amok in the wrong hands (just like golemim). And we must not forget the insistence that "Policymaking ought to be guided by responsible and inclusive moral vision, taking seriously both opportunities and risks, respecting autonomy and individual rights, and showing solidarity with and concern for the interests and dignity of all people around the globe. We must also consider our moral responsibilities towards generations that will exist in the future" (Section 6, Transhumanist Declaration).

But in the next section, the Declaration continues and concludes with this: "We advocate the well-being *of all sentience,* including humans, non-human animals, and *any future artificial intellects, modified life forms, or other intelligence to which technological and scientific advance may give rise"* (Section 7, Transhumanist Declaration).

So, in this world, even the Golem of Prague has rights, just as "future artificial intellects (et al.)" are to enjoy "well-being" due to sentience.

Was the Golem "sentient"? Because the Golem could (temporarily) speak, did it have the "knowledge of good and evil" within it? Because it wanted to be a soldier, did it know that it would die?

The answer is no to both questions, but in the worldview of transhumanism/post-humanism and its growth from post-modernism, the Golem is considered both in possession of human intellect and sentient. The argument advanced is that human-created life forms have the same right to well-being as the rest of created life. I can see that becoming a problem.

But the idea of granting status to life forms created by human means is a profound deviation from the intent of the original Golem story. It obscures the warning it contains which is similarly provided by the story of Prometheus and Mary Shelley's Frankenstein – don't play with fire. You might get burned.

While section six acknowledges the potential for harm, section seven rather chooses to ignore it. At the same time, it implicitly predicts a war for rights on the part of the creatures brought into being by human hands. This philosophical contradiction hints at an agenda to incorporate the golemim of transhumanism into regional and international human rights codes.

Gershom Scholem acknowledged as a leading authority of Kabbalah and Jewish Mysticism, saw it all coming in 1965. This is the year he named one of the first computers in Israel "Golem I."

In the act and naming of the computer, Scholem pre-emptively indicted the future. This stands in the same school of thought as the naming of the sun and moon by God in the Genesis Creation narrative. Reducing the computer to a function that serves humanity, Scholem attached to the innovation creaturely limitations. And no. He didn't do this because he thought he was God. He did this to remind people of God and of the Golem itself. So, the naming of the first computer by Gershom Scholem was both a warning and an indictment.

He understood that the computer had been created to understand only the language of code (numbers), just as the Golem had been created only to operate with the scroll containing the Holy Name in its mouth and only in response to its master (language). Gershom Scholem saw, in 1965, transhumanism's excesses and hubris, naming them as the ultimate terminus of human-created life – the eventual conflict between the life created and the creator.

It's not like the Golem hasn't been pointing the way this whole time. Regardless, some have derived an alternative interpretation that is rooted in the human drive for immortality.

Symbol of a Mystical Community

Moshe Idel has appeared earlier in this book as a source of expertise on Jewish Mysticism, Kabbalah, and the Sefer Yetzirah. To that end, in 1990, he wrote "*Golem: Jewish Magical and Mystical Traditions on the Artificial Anthropoid.*"

In this book, Idel illuminates a far nobler role for the Golem than that of being the prototype for a dystopian future of artificial intelligence and the human desire for eternality – to be unbound by their limitations created humanity. He speculates that the idea of the Golem acted as an icon of status for Jews.

By defining Judaism as the nexus of supernatural abilities, the Golem acts as a symbol of elevation in this model and, with it, the Hebrew language. In fact, Kabbalah, the work of Abraham Abulafia and Joseph Gikatilla and the Sefer Yetzirah (and el Bahir, elevates the Hebrew language to a mystical idiom of extraordinary power, centering it as the language of God and the very substance of Creation.

Perhaps Idel has a point about the Golem. But suppose you look at it from outside the tradition of Judaism. There, the Golem serves only to further "other" the Jewish community, in its uncanniness and in its multifarious creators' disobedience to the prohibition against humans creating life. But it's the curiosity generated by the revelation of such a creature in Jewish lore that provokes fascination and engagement with the source.

And in fascination and curiosity, there is potential.

There is potential for the negative – the claims of blood libel (the theft of Christian babies to produce matzah) that arose against Jews in the Europe of the Middle Ages, for one example. But there is also the potential for the positive. In the exploration of the Golem and its mystical origins, there is a unique opportunity for a profound change in attitude among gentiles, from one of suspicion and contempt (which continue to threateningly exist) to one of acceptance and respect.

Within Judaism, the Golem continues to stand as a call to humility in the face of our creaturely position in the Created Order. We do not stand in place of God but serve God. The Golem is a reminder of what can happen when we stand in the wrong place. That place is taken.

In Jewish Mysticism, though, especially in texts like the Sefer Yetzirah, there is promise and hope. Traditional Judaism has embraced Sefer Yetzirah, and integration that has transformed it and transformed the way Judaism is lived within the tradition and understood outside it.

The Embrace of Mysticism

Jewish Mysticism, once the weird and somewhat wayward cousin of traditional Judaism, has come of age.

Today, books like the Sefer Yetzirah and its fellow Kabbalistic superstar, the Zohar, are considered part of the accepted commentary on Torah, while Isaac Luria's spiritualized presentation of tikkun olam is central to Jewish theology.

Once the rebellious outsider roaming the darkened streets in a black leather jacket, Hassidism now stands as one of the most traditionally engineered sectors of Judaism. And in Jewish Academia, mysticism is growing in prominence.

The academic study of Jewish history, arising in the 19th Century, was embarrassed by Jewish Mysticism. The Jewish Enlightenment (late 18th to early 19th Century), prioritizing integration with Europe's dominant demographic of the time, had worked its rationalistic magic on those who would present a historical picture of the movement of the Jewish Faith through history. There was no place for the Hasidic communities of Europe in this project or for other traditionally Orthodox and devout communities.

It was the Enlightenment that brought together the Hassidim and the Mitnagdim in common cause against the anti-mysticism and overall anti-religiosity of g Haskalah (the Enlightenment) and Maskilim (apologists).

But this attitude was transformed by the work of Gershom Scholem (1897 - 1982). Unconcerned with the struggle inside Judaism in the confrontation of mysticism, Scholem was the first to present the mystical tendency in the Faith as a source of academic exploration, bringing the concepts of the Kabbalah and its books into the public square and into mainstream Judaism.

Other figures must be considered here, besides Scholem, who has helped to change the position of Jewish Mysticism. Martin Buber (1878 - 1965) was a philosopher and writer (and Nobel Laureate) whose I and Thou defined the philosophy of dialogue as a branch of existentialism. Figures heavily influenced Buber's thinking and writing in the Hasidic tradition.

Abraham Joshua Heschel (1907 - 1972) is another key figure in the ascension of Jewish Mysticism and its modern status in Judaism. One of the leading voices in Judaism of the 20th Century, his philosophical works are widely studied in both Judaism and Christianity. Descended from the Hasidic Apter Rav, his work is infused with the mysticism of the sages. Both Buber and Heschel were uniquely focused on the relationship between humanity and the Divine – the whole point of tikkun from the Lurianic perspective.

The Renewal Movement

In Chapter Five, we briefly touched on the Jewish Renewal Movement and the work of Rabbi Zalman Schachter-Salomi. Founding the Renewal Movement in the 1960s (also known as "Four Worlds" Judaism), his desire for the movement was to create a locus for the revitalization of Judaism in response to the ravages of the Holocaust.

Here is probably one of the most potent "evangelists" (after the Lubavitcher Rebbe) for the Kabbalistic approach to spirituality. But Schachter-Salomi was also passionately ecumenical in his approach, inviting those outside Judaism into a deeper experience of God, via mysticism, as understood in the tradition he was raised. Rabbi Schachter-Salomi was from an Ashkenazi Hasidic, Chabad Lubavitch family. While Schachter-Salomi left this tradition in favor of founding Renewal, he is one of the chief proponents of integrating mysticism into the greater tradition of Judaism toward the renewal of the Faith and expressly toward tikkun olam. So, whether he left Chabad or set up another branch that included women, ecstatic prayer, and song as pathways to the Divine union is a matter of opinion.

Today is known as ALEPH: Alliance for Jewish Renewal, Schachter-Salomi's movement continues to impact the greater community, but the impact it has made has led to a wider understanding and acceptance of mysticism as an integral and vibrant part of Judaism, ordaining its own clerical personnel and becoming an enlivening branch of Judaism.

Chabad Lubavitch

When talking about the presence of Jewish Mysticism in the public square through its written documents, no source is more ardently committed to restoring the Jewish spirit than Chabad (an acronym for Chockmah – Binah – Da'a) Lubavitch. Upholding wisdom, understanding, and knowledge, the movement's spiritual roots are firmly rooted in Kabbalah.

Chabad reserves that ardent commitment to Jews alone, rejecting all commentary by secular experts like Gershom Scholem and Martin Buber.

So, while Chabad is bound and determined to share the limitless riches of Kabbalah and the Lubavitcher way of life with Jews outside the mystical tradition, they have no interest in converting anyone to Judaism.

In Israel, their efforts are the subject of much interest and much scrutiny. For instance, their attitude toward the establishment of Israel is historically hostile, and yet, Lubavitchers roam the country, looking for people to lay tefillin (the boxes wrapped on the hands and head) on. Once questioned about his attitude to Zionism, Rabbi Menachem Mendel Schneerson (1902 – 1994) said, "If Israel is a State of Jews, I am not a Zionist. If Israel is a Jewish State, then I am a Zionist."

But unlike other Hasidic groups, like the anti-Israeli Satmar sect, Chabad has made considerable contributions to the life of the nation, even serving in the Israeli Defense Forces in respectable numbers, and Rabbi Schneerson regularly interfaced with Israeli leaders.

At issue is Israel's foundation as a secular state, with early leaders like David Ben Gurion (1876 – 1973) rejecting religious rule for the state. Chabad rejects secularism, but it also rejects the insular approach of the Haredi – the Ultra-Orthodox.

Chabad is a faction affiliated with ultra-Orthodoxy, which believes in reasoned compromise while seeking to be involved at the political level on a moral basis, acting as a "conscience of the nation." The fastest-growing sect of Judaism in the world, Chabad's influence in Israel is of no little interest in our discussion of Sefer Yetzirah in the public square.

While there are over 1 million Haredi in Israel, there are only between 16,000 and 18,000 Chabad households, making their public presence well out of proportion with their demographic presence. Educational opportunities have marked Chabad's contributions in Israel for young people who've grown up in secular households. But Chabad also brings the Holidays to the military, and religious instruction. There is also support for women who've had babies, with the care of the home as the mother recovers from the physical toll of giving birth. While people may chuckle at Chabad's missionary zeal, no one would ever say they haven't contributed to Israeli society.

Sharing Mysticism

One of the greatest cataclysms in the history of cataclysms to ever befall the Jewish people was the Holocaust. And the Lubavitchers were not spared. It was Rabbi Schneerson who breathed new life into the movement. From its degraded, post-war status, Rabbi Schneerson re-visioned Chabad as an enlivening movement within Judaism, making it the most influential of Jewish tendencies.

Outreach was Chabad's focus under Rabbi Schneerson's leadership, and "the Rebbe," as he's known, was a pioneer in pursuing Chabad's outreach to the Jews, sharing with it a Torah-centered lifestyle, rooted in profound spirituality and the realization of the mitzvot.

So much the face of his movement, when he died in 1994, an entire faction in Chabad refused to accept his death, deciding he was the promised Messiah. While this faction persists to this day, most in the movement have abandoned the idea, and Chabad has rejected Messianic claims in the confrontation of the Rebbe.

Schneerson also established education for women and girls, which is a tremendous shift for a Hasidic sect. He considered this to be one of the most important changes in Chabad's mission of spiritual outreach to Jews.

His popularization of the use of tefillim spurred a revival in their use among mainstream Jews. Until this time, their use had been mostly limited to the ultra-observant and ultra-Orthodox.

But some of the Rebbe's greatest achievements were in political and social justice outreach to non-Jews. In the early 80s, Schneerson launched a worldwide campaign to raise awareness of God through the understanding and observance of the 7 Noahide Laws. He believed that adherence to these laws was the basis for all the human rights we enjoy. Specifically:

1. Not worshipping idols

2. Not cursing God

3. Not committing murder

4. Not committing sexual immorality, bestiality, or adultery

5. Not stealing

6. Not to eat flesh torn from an animal still alive

7. The establishment of courts of justice

These seven laws are for all humanity – not just Jews. Those who follow them are considered Righteous Gentiles who will reach the World to Come (Olam Haba). Schneerson knew that these laws represented the basis of repairing humanity's ruptured relationship with God, so without releasing the Kabbalistic genie from the bottle, he encouraged all people to focus on their fidelity the 7 Noahide

Laws. In terms of Kabbalistic impact, bringing more people to the tikkun party is high on the charts.

The Rebbe also advocated for dedicating more funding to solar energy research, nuclear disarmament, and extending foreign aid to developing nations.

Rabbi Schneerson firmly believed that being a righteous person (tzadek) was imperative for Jews and all living people. This was his understanding of how tikkun was to be achieved – by the sanctification of all human life to the project of restoring Creation.

Perhaps more than any other Jewish leader, Rabbi Schneerson dedicated himself to throwing open the doors of Jewish Mysticism and traditional Judaism to the world, to share their common riches. Not for the sake of conversion but for the sake of tikkun, he widened the circle. He did this out of both compassion for those living in darkness and for the reclamation of Creation and the realization of tikkun.

Whether he was the Messiah or not, he brought the world a renewed understanding and appreciation of Judaism through his unique charisma, devoutness, and dedicated scholarship. He found space for those not of the Faith to find a pathway to liberation of the soul from ignorance through education and the rehabilitation of Creation from the brokenness of shevirah. Righteousness and the mysterious balance between Divine omnipotence and Divine love were at the center of the Rebbe's mission.

It could readily be said that Rabbi Schneerson was an international ambassador of Judaism and its role in the satisfaction of a Creation healed of its wounds.

What Is the Golem Pointing At?

In a world of mass media, it's impossible that a book like the Sefer Yetzirah can escape unscathed. It's inevitable that it will be viewed through a variety of lens, some of them distorted by self-interest or self-interested opportunism.

And some will just want to make their own personal Golem. That's also inevitable.

The Sefer Yetzirah lives in many places on the internet, from Christian Cabbalah sites to Chabad to Israeli newspapers, regularly publishing articles related to the book.

And it is studied and mined for evidence and held up as a secret book that holds the key to all that is. This might be true. But what's clear is that the book can be interpreted in many strange, wonderful ways, both illuminating and obscuring.

The Golem is pointing at the central desire expressed in the book, that the 32 pathways be followed, and that the holiness of the Hebrew characters and the definitive quality of numbers might bring us all closer to the longed-for healing of Creation.

With Natural Language Processing standing at the heart of Artificial Intelligence, it seems that another Golem is in the works. This may or not be playing with fire in the Promethean sense. I leave that to the reader. What I do know is that the Golem is pointing.

And as Sefer Yetzirah, the birthplace of the Golem, rises in academic and interfaith prominence, we may yet find in its wisdom a secret thought, wrapped in letters and numbers that brings us to understanding.

The Golem points. But do our eyes follow?

Conclusion

"Wisdom is the level above all division, where everything is a simple unity."

Aryeh Kaplan

Thank you for joining me in this exploration of one of the fascinating books in the canon of Jewish religious literature.

In the Sefer Yetzirah, there are lessons for those willing to bend their heads over an ancient text in the dim light of a candle, drawing from its words the letters, then their derivatives through various means. Arriving at the concealed, Divine spark just beneath the surface of the text, the sage is illuminated by the 32 pathways themselves. This is the gift of Sefer Yetzirah - its demand for intellectual rigor and the spiritual commitment to engage in it. The book is a deliberate challenge to those bold enough to seek its true message.

Without voluminous and studious commentaries arising over time, the Sefirah Yetzirah's meaning might have been entirely lost to us. The towering achievement of this tradition of study and commentary is in its interpretative splendor, redolent with the narratives and lessons of the Torah, while enveloped in mysticism that seeks to penetrate its inner soul.

I hope you've found here much food for thought, and salient information to direct you toward further avenues of study. I highly recommend that you not stop here, as there is a world of reading and exploration about the Sefer Yetzirah's small but mighty contents. In its lessons, there is much wisdom to be had.

The 21st Century has more than enough space for the mystical, especially when it's accompanied by such vibrant intellectual achievement and spiritual ardor. In these post-modern, post-human, post-spiritual times, humanity continues to cry out for the wisdom that delivers us from evil and which unites us to our ultimate source.

Whether you are Jew or gentile, dear readers, I thank you for having shared this journey with me and trust that you'll find good company on your next.

Here's another book by Mari Silva that you might like

MARI SILVA

JEWISH MYSTICISM

The Ultimate Guide to Understanding Kabbalah, Merkabah Mysticism, and Ashkenazi Hasidism

Your Free Gift (only available for a limited time)

Thanks for getting this book! If you want to learn more about various spirituality topics, then join Mari Silva's community and get a free guided meditation MP3 for awakening your third eye. This guided meditation mp3 is designed to open and strengthen ones third eye so you can experience a higher state of consciousness. Simply visit the link below the image to get started.

https://spiritualityspot.com/meditation

References

A Cipher on the the *Sefer Yetzirah*. (n.d.). Www.Rahul.net. Retrieved from
http://www.rahul.net/raithel/ofw/sefer.html

Politecnico di Torino Porto Institutional Repository. (n.d.).
https://www.ijsciences.com/pub/article/498